as in little things...

# AS IN LITTLE THINGS...

Finding Answers to the Great Questions
of Life from Everyday Experiences

Oluwaseun Bayode

*AS IN LITTLE THINGS.* Finding Answers to the Great Questions of Life from Everyday Experiences.

ISBN-13: 979-8-218-32459-9

Library of Congress Control Number: 2023922641

Cover Design: Klassic Designs@ 99designs

Layout Design: Isa Reader

The author can be reached through Asinlittlethings.com

# CONTENTS

# Foreword

There is an old story of a wealthy king who had four wives. He adored the fourth wife and adorned her with rich robes. He treated her to the finest of delicacies and gave her nothing but the best.

He was infatuated with his third wife and relished in showing off her charm to the royals in neighboring kingdoms. However, he feared that she would one day leave him for another.

He enjoyed the company of his second wife. She was his confidant and was always kind, considerate, and patient with him. Whenever the king faced a problem, he could confide in her, and she would help him get through the difficult times.

The king's first wife was more than a loyal partner; she was one with him, ever by his side. She sustained his vigor, without which he would be unable to govern. However, he did not love the first wife. Although she loved him deeply, he had long since taken her for granted and hardly took notice of her anymore!

One day, the king fell ill and knew that his days were numbered. Reflecting on his fate, he had a mournful thought: *I now have four wives with me, but when I die, I will be all alone.*

Thus, he asked the fourth wife, "I have loved you the most, lavished you with the finest clothing, and showered great care over you. Now that I am dying, will you follow me to the grave and keep me company?"

"No way!" replied the fourth wife. She walked away without another word. Her answer cut like a sharp knife right into the king's heart.

The sad king then asked the third wife, "I have loved you all my life. Now that I'm dying, will you follow me to the grave and keep me company?"

"No! Life is too good. When you die, I am going to remarry," she replied.

His heart sank and turned cold.

He then asked the second wife, "I have always turned to you for help, and you have always been there for me. When I die, will you follow me to the grave and keep me company?"

"I am sorry. I cannot help you this time!" she replied. "At the very most, I can only walk with you to your grave."

Her answer struck him like a bolt of lightning, and the king was devastated.

Then a voice called out: "I will go with you. I will always follow you no matter where you go." The king looked up, and there was his first wife. She was skin and bones, as she suffered from malnutrition and neglect.

Deeply grieved, the king said, "I should have taken much better care of you when I had the chance!" He had lavished his attention, wealth, and vigor on all but what was most essential. In his neglect, he had so weakened the best part of himself that he was now filled with regret.

Each of us is like the king of a kingdom that we direct with our thoughts, words, and deeds. Of the king's four wives, the fourth wife represents the physical body. No matter how much effort is spent making it beautiful, the body is temporary and will decompose into dust. The third wife represents possessions, status, and wealth. However much or little we have will eventually be passed on to others. The second wife represents family and friends. No matter how close our relationships, death is an individual odyssey. The first wife stands for the spirit. Often neglected in the pursuit of the many pleasures of life, it is the only part of us that remains after all else fades.

What distinguishes a virtuous king from a vain king? It is his ability to identify the most essential wife and treat her accordingly. If this is done, the other wives will fall seamlessly into place. The king will naturally care for his body and keep it healthy. He will enjoy his possessions responsibly and use them to further the lives of those around him. He will cherish his friends and gain strength from their gatherings.

Like the king in this story, if the spirit in us is ignored, our "other wives" will be deprived of their guidance. Inner chaos will ensue and destroy our well-being. To say "chaos" is no exaggeration. We need only look at the alarming increase in suicides, depression, and mental health issues in our society. To regain our spiritual health is the most important task facing every human being.

Those who perceive the starving first wife in themselves, and wish to strengthen her, often find themselves caught in a labyrinth of human opinions. More than ever, the onslaught of information available today often makes it difficult to find a way out of the maze. Putting aside all we have been taught and conditioned to believe, let us regain trust in our own ability to examine things more clearly and objectively. Upon closer examination of occurrences in our everyday life, certain unfailing spiritual principles will emerge to reveal the wisdom and orderliness of Creation. The answers to the great questions of life need not be a mystery; they often lie amid our everyday experiences. As it is in little things, so it is in the great world of spiritual events.

The stories in this book seek to strengthen the "first wife" in us by shedding light on the countless opportunities offered to us daily for the benefit of our spiritual growth. The purpose of this is to help us consciously experience the love of the Almighty Father in all circumstances. I encourage you to consider carefully and objectively everything presented in this book and to accept only what you confirm to be true from your own experiences.

# PART I

# A GLIMPSE INTO THE NATURE OF THE CREATOR

On a cold January evening, I returned from work to find my brand-new car missing. I was sure I last parked it on the street next to my apartment as I always did. Where could it be? I stood in the street for a few seconds, bewildered. Then I noticed that there were no vehicles on the side of the street where I usually parked my car. I quickly realized that the city must have towed my car. Unbeknownst to me, the city had declared a snow emergency in preparation for an expected overnight storm. When a snow emergency is declared by the city, parking is only allowed on one side of the street to give plow trucks enough room to clear the snow.

Taking public transportation for years, I had no reason to pay attention to the snow emergency rules, and I was not aware of how to sign up to get alerts from the city when a snow emergency is declared. I walked a few miles to the nearest tow shop, where I found my car among other vehicles whose owners had also failed to obey the snow emergency parking restrictions. My ignorance of this rule would cost me a few hundred dollars to release my car from the tow lot that evening. No amount of explanation could void the towing fine. Ignorance of the law is no excuse. A driver has certain rights and responsibilities. The enjoyment of a driver's rights in a civilized society depends on the observance of the rules of the road.

Just as a driver needs to be aware of the driving rules and regulations so must we be aware of the spiritual laws that govern Creation. Let us proceed together in this book on a journey of discovering these spiritual laws as well as the rights and responsibilities of the human spirit. But first, we must acknowledge the existence of a Divine guidance. We must also trust in the abilities we have been granted to recognize this Divine guidance and, thus, find our true path. The following story helps to illustrate the importance of acknowledging and connecting to our Source.

In need of cash for admittance to a poetry slam competition at the Green Mill Jazz Club, Samira stops at a Bank of America ATM. She inserts her card and enters her personal identification number (PIN). "Incorrect PIN" flashes on the screen. "What is my PIN? I know it begins with 1986, but what are the last two numbers?" She tries 198605 but gets the same incorrect PIN message.

The people standing in line behind her are getting restless. In her panic, she turns around to ask the man directly behind her for his help with her PIN. The stranger pulls her aside and kindly tells her, "Nobody here can help you with your PIN. If you cannot remember it, call Bank of America and they will remind you of the numbers."

*✱*

Samira's questioning this man, of course, seems silly. But if you think of this bank as the source of *spiritual* wealth, it serves to illustrate an important point. Would we look to others for specific guidance to access the wealth that lies within us? Each person's spiritual path is different. Specific advice that helps one person may be harmful to another. The best advice is that which helps the receiver to see more clearly, thus enabling her to find her path for herself more quickly. By directing Samira to Bank of America, the stranger gives her a lifelong anchor she can always cling to in her hour of need. He reminds her that she can go *directly* to the "Source;" this alone can give the young woman lasting confidence. Should she ever lose her way or become confused to the point of forgetting her PIN, she is comforted by the thought that her bank exists. Without this knowledge, she would go from place to place seeking help from sources that cannot possibly give her what she truly seeks.

Let us not overlook a seemingly minor but important point. To find her PIN, she must first acknowledge that she needs help finding it. To receive, we must first ask. How often do we waste our precious time on earth just enduring life rather than fully and consciously tapping into the great spiritual gifts slumbering within us? We keep doing what we have always done without ever pausing to question seriously if a more fulfilling path exists.

As children, we are constantly running and hopping about with excitement. But as we get older that excitement for life that should drive us on to purposeful and fascinating work often declines. An earnest effort is then required to get that excitement back. Growing up in Nigeria, my family lived on a simple compound that enclosed about thirty bungalows. We knew almost every family on the compound, and I never lacked friends to play with. Our electricity was inconsistent, so my sister and I, along with the other kids in the neighborhood, had to create games to entertain ourselves. We often lacked water, too, so we kids had the adventurous task of walking across a half mile of marshy land to fetch water to use at home. There were planks and rocks that we skillfully had to navigate to avoid stepping into the boggy, frog-infested marsh. It was all a game to us.

As is the case in the development of every child, the innocence of my childhood was soon replaced by the awareness of the reality of the surroundings beyond my home. When I went to boarding school at the age of ten, I became increasingly aware of the suffering that existed all around me. The sight of young children begging for spare change on major roadways, under the scorching rays of the early afternoon sun, made one wonder how all this suffering was possible in a land blessed with great wealth. Life seemed much more difficult than I felt it needed to be. Shouldn't the primary function of any public institution in society be to help men and women enjoy a more meaningful existence? I was confused as to why this was not the case.

In school, I crammed all kinds of information into my young brain that I could hardly connect to my real life.

Meanwhile, I sought in vain the knowledge of something I could not explain at the time. I did not understand it then, nor could I articulate my feelings, but I wanted to find that activity that made my spirit come alive. As I progressed from high school to college, the realization that I would soon have to decide on a career path became apparent. Like some of my classmates, I had no idea what I wanted to do but hoped I would figure it out along the way.

After graduating, I accepted a job offer from a bank. And so began my career in the financial services industry. A few years into my career, after the initial excitement had waned, I found myself lost and lacking a direction for my life. I had "lost my PIN" and needed help finding it. My job was not the problem. It enabled me to support myself financially and gave me enough time to pursue personal interests outside of work. The problem was that I did not know what to pursue. I had to find something meaningful to do with my life outside of work. My education gave me the tools to make a living. To live well, however, I would require higher guidance.

Months of prayer and reflection over many long walks at the park led me to an insight on November 29, 2013. On this Friday night after work, I watched a video, most of which I can hardly recall, but the speaker mentioned that he had created a website for a project he was working on. There was something in that moment that made me act immediately. I don't even remember the speaker's name. All I remember were his comments about creating a website. I spent the next hours learning how to create a website and completed the design of the website just before dawn the next morning. The website would serve as my platform to post short stories that I hoped would help me and my readers draw useful spiritual lessons from everyday experiences. Lessons that would help us discover and consciously adjust ourselves to the rhythm of the natural laws, thereby enabling the spiritual forces in Creation to work for our benefit rather than to our detriment. At last, I had discovered the activity that made my spirit come alive. I had regained my PIN and was actively tapping into the inner wealth bestowed upon me by the Almighty Creator.

With this new energy, I no longer dreaded the work week. My experiences at work became the inspiration for new stories. I paid closer attention to everything around me to discern patterns that revealed spiritual principles, and to my amazement, I realized that the answers to some of the great life questions we seek present themselves in simple life occurrences. I did not know what would come of the stories or even if anyone would read them. All I knew was that I felt most fulfilled when engaged in the process of writing. I did not have all the answers, but I had found something important. I had found a direction!

Each of us has talents with which we can improve ourselves and serve our community, but we often deprive these talents of the oxygen they need to awaken by pursuing paths that do not belong to us. To feel dissatisfied about your occupation is a warning sign telling you to re-examine and act before it is too late. It is not always necessary to change careers, but it is necessary to find time to identify and consistently engage in activities that elicit inner joy. The Almighty wants us to live full and happy lives. If we are not fully alive and engaged in purposeful work that aligns with our talents, it is clear proof that we have closed ourselves to that spark that makes life enjoyable. When we are fully engaged in purposeful work that aligns with our unique talents, we are connected to the radiations of the Creator of the Universe. Now tell me, what reward comes anywhere close to being connected to Him who has it all?

But, you might argue, there are many celebrated, successful people who engage in purposeful work aligned with their talents, yet some of them look like they have lost their PIN. They are inwardly unbalanced. Perhaps some of them, in extreme cases, are even suicidal. What about these people?

# Our talents are not given to us merely for the sake of accomplishments that improve the lives of others or make us wealthy.

They are given to us to develop spiritually. To discover the Will of the Creator by putting our talents into action for the improvement of our society. In the process of engaging in purposeful work that improves the lives of others, we will recognize certain spiritual principles that reveal the Will of the Creator. This Will is not for the Creator's benefit; rather, it is for the benefit of our joy and welfare. We are spiritual beings and will therefore remain unsatisfied until we discover and apply these spiritual principles. Life on earth only gains real value through striving upward spiritually. Accomplishing great things with our talents is not the end goal but a means through which we recognize the Will of the Creator. A small farmer who understands the spiritual law of sowing and reaping through his experience working in the field, and sees the Will of The Creator in this, is more spiritually advanced than the world's greatest architect who does not recognize the Will of the Creator in the mathematical principles he uses in his work every day. Our purpose in life will be addressed in greater detail in the second part of the book.

No logical person would assume that anything in our material world created itself. Why would anyone then assume that Creation could magically appear without being preceded by events set in motion by a wiser, unseen Creator? Perhaps, it is the false understanding of the nature of the Creator disseminated by humanity throughout history that is responsible for this assumption. But is that reason enough to abandon the logical reality of the existence of a Creator? We need not throw the baby out with the bathwater but instead learn to listen within. As with Samira, should we ever lose our way or become confused to the point of forgetting our purpose, the Creator's help is available to us if we are open to receiving it. The increasing understanding of the nature of the Creator alone can give us lasting confidence. Without it, every experience would seem like a random occurrence hanging in isolation without a cause. In ignorance, we simply accept whatever comes our way without realizing the spiritual wealth that lies within each of us to shape our inner and outer environment. The foundation is thus laid that the awareness of the existence of the Creator is paramount for any enduring confidence throughout life.

Next, let's consider this question: *What is the nature of the Creator?* At least what little of His nature that can be perceived from the observation of our surroundings.

# CHAPTER 1

# The Sublime in Everyday Life

*Greatness is never obtrusive. It works in silence,
seeking no recognition. This is why it is not easily
perceived and recognized. Like the mountain, it towers
up in its vastness, so that those in its immediate vicinity,
who receive its shelter and shade, do not see it. Its
sublime grandeur is only beheld as they recede from it.*

— *James Allen*

Consider the massive sphere of hot gas that we call the sun. How many earths do you imagine would fit in the sun? Take a guess (no googling). If you guessed somewhere in the ballpark of one million, congratulations! That's correct. Approximately one million earths would fit into that yellow ball you see in the sky. How great must be the creator of such a powerful star! We cannot begin to comprehend this greatness. No earthly illustration can come close to depicting the great gap between us and the Almighty.

The following tale about a young boy's perception of the Roman ruler Julius Caesar isn't comparable, but it at least gives some perceptive of the naivety often displayed in our conversations about our relationship to the Creator.

A young father tells his four-year-old son that Caesar will be passing through their province in a few days. Seeing no sign of excitement from his son, he tells him about the Roman sovereign and the absolute power he wields over his subjects. "He rules most of the world."

Not comprehending the scope of the world, the four-year-old would simply understand it to be bigger than his home. And as his father was the head of the house, then this Caesar person must be the next level higher, for he governs a wider expanse.

"So, will Caesar join us for dinner?" he asked his father.

Bursting into laughter, the father shook his head. "No, son. We will have to go to him if we wish to see him."

Smiling, he watched his son run off to play. Then the thought occurred to him that it was foolish to expect his son to understand the office of Caesar. How could he? He was only a child and lacked knowledge of the many levels of government between himself and Caesar.

*\*\**

Just as a four-year-old cannot truly understand the concept of a Caesar, how can we glean even a faint idea of the Sublimity of the Creator of the universe when we can't comprehend the many levels of Creation between ourselves and our Creator? Childlike faith is no longer sufficient for humanity today; we must become aware of the many levels of Creation to gain an appreciation of the Greatness and Sublimity of the Creator. In our naivety, we skip worlds of incomprehensible distances beyond the highest spiritual realm of the perfect human spirits when we claim divinity in man. Divine is not the same as spiritual; it stands much higher.

We sense the immense potential we have within us to shape our environment, but we err in calling this potential "Divine" or "a part of God." The power of God flows through us, just as it flows through everything in Creation, but not God himself. Just as a magnifying glass can direct the concentrated power of the sun to burn a piece of paper, so do we channel the power of the Creator that sustains us for good or evil. The magnifying glass does not possess the power of the sun; it simply directs a tiny fraction of its power. Any more than a small fraction of the sun's rays would destroy the magnifying glass; it cannot bear it. The ability of the human spirit to guide a tiny fraction of Divine power through our thoughts, words, and deeds is in itself tremendous, but it is not the same as possessing Divine power within ourselves. There is an immense gulf between us and the Creator. This gulf is unfathomable! We can only gain access to Him by being in resonance with the radiations that emanate from Him.

Our words and expressions are powerful; therefore, they should be chosen thoughtfully. Behind every word is a living concept. Take, for example, the word "awesome." When the word was first recorded in 1590, it was defined as "profoundly reverential." Its meaning was limited to the context of worship. By 1961, four centuries later, the word had been redefined for colloquial usage and used to express "impressiveness." Today, we hear the word "awesome" so frequently that it no longer has much value. The original meaning of the word and its sacred connotation has been tarnished and degraded through common usage.

In this light, consider what has happened to the word "God." How often do you hear this holiest of words used daily in response to the most trivial incident? We have lost reverence for the Creator and don't realize the damage we do to ourselves by this. On the other hand, when the word "God" is used with the appropriate reverence, it fills us with confidence and strength. The confidence this holy word instills in us creates a spiritual bridge through which we can receive strength in our hour of need. With the debasement of this word, however, we risk losing access to the Creator through its use. Robbed of its sacred meaning through careless and inappropriate usage, it then becomes just an empty sound lacking any power.

There is a reason why one of the Ten Commandments warns us against using the Lord's name in vain. Do you remember Aesop's fable "The Boy Who Cried Wolf"? The boy was warned not to cry "wolf" if there was no wolf in sight, but he did not listen and tried to fool the villagers with false alarms. When a wolf actually showed up, the boy's cry was meaningless because the villagers no longer took him seriously. He was left abandoned in his hour of need. We will face a similar fate if we do not heed the warning of this commandment.

Reverence for the Creator may not happen overnight.

# Genuine reverence for the Creator cannot be a forced intellectual exercise. It is the natural result of an increasing awareness of His sublimity.

As your knowledge of the Creator's works expands, so too will your reverence expand and deepen. You will no longer use His name casually or think that you have any part of God within you. Even in our perfected state in paradise, we are not on the same level with the Creator. His power flows through us and sustains us, but we do not have Him within us. In the book *In the Light of Truth: The Grail Message* by Abd-ru-shin, the author provides guidance that makes it possible for a human being to gain an increased awareness of the incomprehensible Greatness and Sublimity of the Almighty Creator. We will refer to this book in a later chapter.

Even the little we know of the universe through science is enough to leave us speechless and in wonderment of its Creator's sublimity. Let us return to our earlier discussion about our earth's star, the sun. Its massive size alone leaves us in awe, not to mention the hundreds of billions of other stars in our galaxy, the Milky Way. Hundreds of billions! Can you imagine that? Pause for a moment and reflect on this: The Milky Way is just one of many billions of galaxies in the universe. Looking in any direction, the universe goes on and on for incomprehensive distances! This greatness is too much for a human being to understand. We cannot truly grasp this sublimity, yet there is so much more that is beyond the range of our most powerful telescopes. The increasing awareness of the Creator's sublimity naturally strengthens our reverence towards Him and bolsters trust in the abilities we possess as His creatures.

# CHAPTER 2

# Perfection Hidden in Plain Sight

What speaks to the soul escapes
our measurements.
— *Alexander von Humboldt*

The more we understand our natural surroundings or the Laws of Nature, the more miraculous it all seems. In my birth city of Lagos, Nigeria, where I spent most of my childhood, ants  roaming around was a common sight. A single ant colony can consist of over twenty million ants. I have never known anyone to enjoy the company of ants, me included. They are usually a nuisance to us, and we are quick to declare their worthlessness by killing them. This attitude changes when we learn how they aerate the soil, improve soil chemistry, and disperse seeds to safer, more nutrient-rich habitats. Everything has a purpose that serves the whole, even a tiny ant.

An increasing awareness of the perfection behind the arrangement of all that surrounds us is an essential part of being alive.

Without it, we would continue to see ourselves as the center of the universe, thus putting ourselves at odds with the natural rhythm of the whole. We are simply creatures in Creation. Like the ants, we too have our role to play in supporting the natural rhythm of Creation. If we abandon the path prescribed for us by higher guidance, chaos and confusion will be the result.

A coarse representation of this is given in the following story about a traffic accident.

On her early morning jog, Adanna hears a loud crash on the road and finds herself a witness to a horrific car accident. A driver trying to beat the red light had sped up and lost control of the vehicle when he attempted to avoid a car coming from the opposite direction. "Why didn't he just wait!" she yells.

Traffic on the road slowed to a crawl as the state police and medical staff arrived at the scene. After providing her statement to the police, Adanna sadly walks home in reflection. The sight of the driver being ejected from his vehicle and lying in a pool of blood on the side of the road had disturbed her greatly. "Why didn't he just wait?" she asks herself.

Ten miles back, Gerald sits in his white Tesla Model Y and is growing increasingly agitated by his lack of progress. *There is never any traffic on this road. What could have happened?* he wonders.

Gerald finally gets close enough to see the cause of the gridlock. His agitation is mellowed by a kind thought for the victims of the accident. On reflection, he wonders how the bad decision of one man could harm others and bring hundreds of vehicles on a major road to a halt.

*✲*

Those who understand the purpose of traffic lights respect its wisdom. They know that obedience to this law guarantees order and safety to all road users. By analogy, we can see in every aspect of life how the wisdom of the Creator rules the universe. Take, for example, the perfect arrangement of the human body. Each organ works harmoniously with the rest of the body in the service of the whole. Observe how insects work together with flowers in the pollination process. Notice how one creature's waste is another's food. Behold how the majestic oceans regulate the earth's climate, like the human circulatory system.

# All around us stand witnesses to the perfection and omnipotence of The Creator.

His wisdom is simply breathtaking, and we would be wise to learn from the observation of our surroundings. Biomimicry, the design practice that learns from and mimics the strategies found in nature to solve human environmental and health problems, is a welcome development. For example, the Eastgate Centre in Harare, Zimbabwe's largest office and shopping complex, was built without a conventional air-conditioning system, yet its temperature remains regulated year-round because the building design was inspired by the self-cooling system used by termites to keep their mounds cool. This approach resulted in a significant reduction in energy consumption, carbon dioxide emissions, and energy costs.

We sometimes look to Nature for inspiration in the design and invention of products, but rarely do we look to her for guidance on how to live a more harmonious life. For example, constant movement is a fundamental requirement for renewal and survival. This is the law of movement. A stream that stops flowing will soon lose its vitality and become a stagnant breeding ground for insects that transmit dangerous diseases. We see similar ill-fated consequences to the human body if blood flow is hampered. The same applies to the earth, should it stop rotating around the sun. In its movement, everything in Nature contributes something to the whole, either voluntarily or involuntarily. It must!

Closely linked with the law of movement is the law of equilibrium. As human beings, we must breathe out carbon dioxide in order to breathe in oxygen. Food intake is balanced by waste elimination. Work and rest are required for a healthy body. The law of equilibrium is upheld and furthered by harmony, which lies in the fulfillment of all the Primordial Laws of Creation. If we truly understand the wisdom of these Laws of Creation, we will adjust ourselves voluntarily to this constant movement in all areas of our lives. If we do not flow with the spirit of the movement that permeates Nature, we become stagnant and susceptible to all kinds of illnesses. A woman who hoards her seeds and refuses to give them to the earth will eventually forfeit both the seeds and the harvest. The same applies to our abilities; undeveloped talents will be lost. A man who hoards the money he has saved and refuses to invest in a reasonable enterprise or his education will watch that money depreciate over time. But a man who, depriving himself of short-term comforts, spends the little he has on developing his small farm and is confident of a good harvest in six months is on his way to claiming all the good things that Creation offers him. Rapid, unnatural movement is just as dangerous as being stagnant. Change in Nature is gradual and rhythmic. Night gradually turns into day. Herein lies an insight that will protect many from deceptive schemes promising quick spiritual or physical transformation. The consequences of these schemes often don't show up until much later.

Everything must be wisely put to use; everything must be in constant, steady movement, otherwise, it will decay. This is just one example of the guidance we are afforded if we take the time to patiently observe Nature and adjust ourselves to her laws, such as the law of movement. If we adapt ourselves accordingly, the power propelling all movement in Nature will strengthen us spiritually and physically. Should we neglect to do this, we will stand helpless.

Through science, we have a glimpse into the extensive preparations over billions of years that had to precede our arrival on earth as human beings. Do you ever wonder what keeps your heart beating? We are completely dependent on the Creator for our existence. We can hardly comprehend all the events that make it possible for us to take a single breath. The order and precision of Nature give evidence of its Creator's perfection. Having created a perfect work, He need not interfere. In prayer, we sometimes think that the Creator personally and arbitrarily grants us what we seek but that is not so. In His perfect Creation, everything we need for our growth and supreme happiness has been provided. With the right attitude, we simply obtain a connection to those regions where the help we seek can be proffered. Everything flows according to the established rhythm of Creation, also known as the laws of Nature.

When we disregard the natural rhythm of Creation in favor of our ideas, gridlock, chaos, and devastation will be the result. Earthly laws established by the state can be flawed and are not the same as the immutable Laws of Creation, but in the case of traffic lights, we can easily see their benefit in maintaining order at intersections. Individuals who break this traffic law not only affect themselves but also sometimes disrupt the progress of those in their environment. Those caught in traffic gridlock due to a car accident would not blame the mayor of the city for the accident but rather the person who caused the accident by disregarding the traffic lights. If that is so, why then do we question the perfection of the Creator in view of the suffering and chaos caused by human beings? Perhaps, one may think, the Creator should interfere and immediately punish all those who cause suffering to others. Ah! but who among us is innocent of this offense? Keep in mind that causing others to suffer is not limited to physical harm. It also includes reputational and emotional harm caused by unkindness and lack of self-control. Secretly harboring selfish desires at the expense of others is also included here. Were the Creator to immediately destroy all those who cause suffering, who among us would remain?

# CHAPTER 3

# Mercy and Patience Abound

Even after all this time, the sun never says to the earth,
"you owe me." Look what happens with a love like
that. It lights up the whole sky
— *Hafiz*

Look around you, dear friend. Observe all the material objects in your midst. Your clothes, shoes, furniture, cell phone, car, house, etc. The raw materials for every one of these objects were in existence long before we discovered their applications and benefits. All the ingredients had long been prepared, waiting for us to put them to use for our sustenance and the ennoblement of the earth. When you really look at the abundance that is offered to us, do you ever wonder how it is that we came to deserve all this? We just take it for granted that the sun will shine tomorrow as it has done for billions of years. We take it for granted that the oxygen needed for our survival will be made available. We take it for granted that the soil will continue to yield crops.

We take from Nature daily and enjoy many of her gifts, but we're often oblivious to her great law which ordains that the right to take lies in giving alone.

The enjoyment of rights lies in the fulfillment of duties. Like a spoiled child who takes for granted the solicitude of his parents and expects ever more blessings without thinking of his duties toward his parents. So have we carried on for a long time. And yet the Creator has been merciful and patient with us.

Consider the following story of a people who went astray despite the meticulous guidance of their king.

There was once a magnificent kingdom in the higher realms, infinitely higher and much brighter than the earth.

The inhabitants of this luminous kingdom lived in harmony according to the established order of the king, which was anchored in love, purity, and justice. Some of the children, however, could not bear the luminous light prevalent in this realm. They could not adjust their eyes to the great brightness of this realm; therefore, they were blind to all the beautiful activities enjoyed by everyone around them.

In his love for these children, the king extended his kingdom to include a lower, less luminous realm, which until then had been devoid of any life. This was done to make it possible for them to develop their senses and grow strong in this realm far away from the great light. And one day they would return to the higher realm as fully matured members of society.

Guides were sent ahead to prepare the lower realm for the little ones, and they would then teach the children how to live according to the noble ways of the king. From the guides, the little ones learned about the land, fire, water, and air. They learned the sacred art of hunting to feed themselves. They learned how to extract fiber from plants to clothe themselves and how to carve tree trunks into useful tools. Closely watched over by the guides, they also enjoyed the bounty and protection of the king and lacked for nothing.

As their knowledge expanded, they began to grow conscious of the talents bestowed upon them by the king. Some of the clever ones began enjoying the admiration they received from the others who looked up to them for guidance. In time, conceit reared its head, and these clever ones began attributing their success solely to their intelligence. Long forgotten was the fact that every discovery made by these little ones would not have been possible without the foundational knowledge from the higher kingdom mediated to them through the guides. These children slowly began corrupting the others and, in time, the guides were no longer sought after by them because they thought they knew best. Centuries of selfishness, greed, and misery followed.

Seeing the destruction that lay ahead for these people along their chosen path, the king sent great messengers to all corners of the lower realm to remind them of the way back to the higher realm, which was the sole purpose of their sojourn in the lower realm. But the evil had become so strong and pervasive that even the messengers' influence was merely transient. Shortly after the messengers left, the people distorted their teachings and created religions in the names of these messengers.

Yet some of these people yearned for the knowledge of the king and the way back to the higher realm. For the sake of these few, the king sent his most powerful envoy. In all his majesty and indescribable power, the envoy descended to the lower realm to show the way out of the darkness. "Love thy neighbor," he said. However, his great love was returned with hatred. The people of the lower realm were so used to their ways of strife and selfishness that his teaching became irksome to them. He, who had come to them out of love from the highest of heights, was brutally murdered by the little people of the lower realm.

And yet, the king temporarily left the door open for those of the lower realm who honestly strove to live according to the eternal principles of love, purity, and justice. Despite the continual failure of the undeserving people who, for millennia, continued to spread discord, he still allowed them to breathe.

What great mercy! What unimaginable patience!

\*\*\*

Pause for a moment and reflect on how merciful and patient the Creator has been with us. As with the earlier example of the traffic accident caused by a driver's unwillingness to heed the guidance of the traffic lights, our decision to ignore the guidance of the Creator not only affects us but also affects other creatures.

According to a study reported by *The Guardian* in 2018, the world's 7.6 billion people represent only 0.01 percent of all living things. And since the dawn of civilization, we have caused the loss of an estimated 83 percent of all wild mammals and half of plant life on earth. Of all the mammals on earth today, 96 percent are livestock and humans; only 4 percent are wild mammals. Seventy percent of the bird population are chicken and poultry, and only 30 percent are wild birds. We have been blindly exploiting natural resources for food and profits at the expense of all other living things. We have been stripping the earth of its protective covering and destroying ecosystems that we ourselves depend on for survival. Creatures are suffering or becoming extinct because of our shortsighted actions. This is just some of the visible evidence on earth of our deviation from the prescribed path designed to lead us back to the luminous kingdom. The unseen spiritual implications are likely even more severe.

Nevertheless, all is not lost. The awareness of His mercy and patience should spur us to redouble our efforts to learn and adjust ourselves to His Will. Do you remember the famous story of the prodigal son? The son asked his father for his inheritance and ended up spending it all recklessly in a distant country. A severe famine arose in that country, and the son had to resort to begging for food. He thought of his father's servants who had more than enough food to eat, while here he was, starving in a foreign land. Humbled by his difficulties, he returned home to seek his father's forgiveness and asked to be treated as one of his father's hired servants. While the son was still a long way off, his father saw him and ran to embrace him. He welcomed him home and threw a big party to celebrate the return of his lost son.

The elder son who had remained with the father was upset. He had obediently served his father but had never received such an extravagant welcome. He shared his thoughts with his father. Do you remember his father's response?

"Son, you are always with me, and all that is mine is yours."

This parable offers us an insight into the spiritual workings in Creation. It is not merely an earthly story. "All that is mine is yours." What does this mean? When we return to the path to our spiritual home and adjust ourselves to the Creator's Will, we become like those who never strayed away and remained open to receiving all the blessings made available to them by the Creator.

We may resonate with the elder son's sentiment. After all, why should the lost son receive more than the obedient elder son? We feel this way because the intellect can only think in terms of finite resources. If the lost son gets more, it must mean the elder son will receive less. "All that is mine is yours." If we limit this sentence to the earthly, we cannot appreciate its value. Seen from a spiritual perspective, however, we see that the resources of the Creator are infinite. When we align with His ways, we are open to receiving all that has been provided for our well-being and happiness.

This can be compared to plugging a device into an electric socket. It does not matter how short a period it is plugged in. As long as it is plugged in, it will receive just as much electrical current as similar devices that have always been plugged in. The same applies to us in relation to the power of the Creator. Like the younger son, we will have to face the consequences of our errors. But if we mature through our experiences, we will be worth just as much in the eyes of the Creator as those who never soiled themselves with guilt. In other words, once we are rehabilitated, our criminal records are expunged.

If we look deeper into the parables of Christ, we will discover principles that depict a spiritual process. Several deep lessons are often packed within a short parable. One of the lessons we can draw from the story of the prodigal son is that it reminds us of our luminous spiritual home. We need not be unhappy and destitute in a foreign land. The choice to return home is an option. What profound mercy and patience!

CHAPTER 4

# The Language of Creation

## Justice and Love

*The visible world is a daily miracle, for those who have eyes and ears*
— *Edith Warton*

To convey my thoughts intelligibly through the medium of my laptop, it is necessary to at least have a basic understanding of how the machine works. If I hit the "K" key on the keyboard in my attempt to type the word "Love," and then complain to you that my laptop can't spell, you would either laugh uncontrollably or advise that I go see a psychiatrist. Unless I override the logic of the keyboard, I will never be able to get the "K" key to type the letter "L." Imagine the frustration if I continue trying to get the letter "L" from the "K" key. It is much the same in life. The machinery of Creation in its wonderful weaving has the sole purpose of helping us, so long as we do not obstruct it by childishly squandering the power given to us.

We cannot override the Laws of Nature so we must learn to understand its language to avoid needless frustration in our lives.

Once, long ago, there was a large kingdom governed by the greatest of kings. The king lived far away in the capital of the land, and most people had never seen him. They only experienced his nature through the impact of his laws on their lives. The king so loved his people that he made the realization of their deepest aspirations possible through his laws. It enabled the people to receive abundantly whatever they aspired for.

To make this possible, the king had a plethora of servants that traversed the vast realm collecting the aspirations of every dweller. The servants planted each person's aspiration in the realm of thoughts and wove threads that connected each person to their aspiration. Like an umbilical cord, which is the baby's lifeline to its mother, the thread was the channel that sustained each aspiration. Every thought a person had about their aspiration passed through the thread and nurtured the aspiration planted in the realm of thoughts. These thoughts were the fuel that brought about the maturity and realization of their earnest aspiration. In this land, just as the harvest sprang from the seeds planted, so did each person's circumstance spring from the seeds of their thoughts.

Two strangers from a faraway land heard about the great king and journeyed to this land of love and prosperity. The first stranger was amazed by what he saw. It seemed to him that everyone lived for the joy of others. The greed and jealousy so prevalent in his homeland were absent here. Gratitude so filled him that he dropped down on his knees, whispering words of thanks to the distant king.

For the second stranger, however, the beauty and abundance of the land awakened greed within him. A few months after settling, he began running into difficulties. His house collapsed during a storm, and his crops struggled to yield. "What kind of horrible land is this? I don't have enough food. Where is the love of this king everyone talks about? Does He even exist?" The man could not see how his thoughts of scarcity and greed were fueling his unfavorable condition.

He thought of his fellow countryman who was always cheerful and decided to speak with him. "How come everything works in your favor in this country? What is your secret?"

He laughed in reply. "Secret? There is no secret. I have simply come to realize that the greatest joy lies in serving others. Because the more I help others, the greater is my joy."

The radiance on his face as he spoke these words did not escape the notice of his friend. The man now understood completely and began a new life of service.

Gradually, he too began helping at every opportunity, and he received help in return. He realized that he had been the cause of his suffering, for he reaped what he had sowed. The king had not changed, and his law had remained inviolable. The change in this man's circumstance was attributable solely to the change in his attitude. He was glad for this recognition and gave thanks for it.

***

How can we gain insight into the nature of the Creator if we have no physical access to Him? By observing how His laws work within the realm of our daily experiences. Take the example of a mango seed. A mango seed can only yield mango fruits; never would it yield oranges. It also does not just yield one mango but a multitude of mangoes. In this simple example, a glimpse into the nature of the Creator is revealed. Justice and love are foundational elements of the Creator's nature.

Let us begin with justice. The fruit we harvest will always be the same as the kind of seed planted. In other words, we reap what we sow. We are part of Nature; therefore, we are subject to this same law. Our thoughts, words, and deeds are seeds we constantly sow. The mature fruits of these seeds will eventually return to us. We cannot escape the reality of this spiritual process. This means that whatever we do to or for others, we in effect do to or for ourselves. We might doubt this because we don't always see the results immediately. But just as different fruit seeds take different amounts of time to develop, so it is with the seeds of our volition.

While looking outside the window from the third floor of my office building one spring afternoon, a colleague of mine witnessed a minor accident in the parking lot and excitedly informed everyone in his vicinity. I hurriedly jumped up from my cubicle and headed toward the window. A driver had hit a stationary vehicle in his attempt to park his vehicle. Looking down from my third-floor window, I could see the anxiety on the man's face as he inspected the extent of the damage to the other vehicle and looked around to see if anyone had witnessed the accident. There was no one else in the parking lot, but he had no idea that we were watching him from above. He got in his vehicle and drove away from the scene of the accident, but then he drove back to take another look at the dented vehicle. I could sense the inner battle raging within this man—should he do the right thing and leave a note with his contact information on the windshield or attempt to flee from his responsibility? My colleagues and I watched hopefully to see if this man would leave a note. Unfortunately, he drove away and parked at the far end of the parking lot and then made his way across the lot into the office building. We did not know who this man was, so my colleague who had first witnessed the accident and called our attention to it went to the parking lot to get the man's license plate number. He reported the accident to office security. The man may have thought he could avoid responsibility for his actions, but by doing so he had made things much worse for himself.

\*\*\*

The man's actions in this story may have a lesson for us about true justice. Are actions and thoughts that we assume are unseen by others on earth being recorded above and awaiting us?

We may agree that it is just when good is rewarded and evil is punished. But it is an error to expect the results within our timeline. In his book *How Can God Allow Such Things*, Dr. Richard Steinpach states: "In all events our inability to see the connection between cause and effect merely proves the inadequacy of our ability to judge and not the absence of justice." Is this true? How many times have we passed judgment or expressed an opinion about an event only to find out later that our assumptions were based on incomplete facts?

Nothing gets lost, everything is working and developing at its own perfectly designed pace. This spiritual process is explained in the book mentioned earlier, *In the Light of Truth: The Grail Message* by Abd-ru-shin. The author states:

> "Try it, for your thoughts are the messengers you send forth, which return heavily laden with similar thought-forms, good or evil as the case may be. This actually happens! Remember that your thoughts are realities that shape themselves spiritually, often becoming forms outliving the earth-life of your body, then much will become clear to you.

Thus it is quite rightly said: "For their works will pursue them!" Thought creations are works which will one day await you! Which form light or dark rings around you, which you must traverse in order to enter the spiritual world. Neither protection nor intervention can help in this, because the decision lies with you. Therefore you yourself must take the first step in everything. This is not difficult; it lies solely in the volition, which expresses itself through thoughts. Thus you carry heaven or hell within you."

You are free to decide, but you are then irrevocably subject to the consequences of your thoughts, of your volition! You yourselves create these consequences, and that is why I exhort you:

Keep the hearth of your thoughts pure, by so doing you will bring peace and be happy!"

Everything we see with our physical eyes on earth is simply the manifestation of an unseen spiritual process. A thought, an idea, a mental picture must precede every action. Even the slightest movement of a finger requires the unseen spiritual energy that animates the body and directs the brain to send motor signals through the spinal cord to muscles around the finger. It all happens so fast that it appears instantaneous. All we do is give direction to this spiritual energy with our volition and the body automatically executes the command. Every effect has a starting point, a cause.

In the same manner, our current circumstance is the result of our thoughts. Just as our body responds to our volition, our outer environment responds to our thoughts, words, and deeds. We often lack the calmness to see the connection between cause and effect in our lives, but we inevitably shape both our inner and outer environment. The earnest desire to connect cause and effect will enable us to develop the awareness to see the connection in certain aspects of our lives. As a test case, begin to speak only of the good you see in others, and you will quickly see its impact on your elevated state of being. Justice maintains order. It gives to each person his due.

A question that often arises on this topic of justice is how to explain the grossly different circumstances into which babies are born. If the Creator is just, why is it that some babies are born in palaces while others are born in slums? Here again, I quote Dr. Richard Steinpach's words to give us guidance for our own investigation of justice: "In all events, our inability to see the connection between cause and effect merely proves the inadequacy of our ability to judge and not the absence of justice." Is it possible that we have all been on earth before and are born into the exact circumstances which we created for ourselves through our past thoughts, words, and actions? Or do you think the family we are born into is just random? We would not expect arbitrariness from a just earthly king, so how can we expect it from the Creator of the magnificent Creation? What can be surmised from everything known about the laws of the universe is that there must be a logical order of cause and effect, even with births.

Let's not go into further detail about reincarnation, since the purpose of this book is to point out how little things in our everyday lives reveal a spiritual process that can help us better understand the big life questions. I only mention it to stimulate reflection on the common question as to why the Creator allows babies to be born into dire circumstances.

We have talked about justice. Now let's turn our attention to love. Using our mango seed analogy, we see justice revealed in the fact that a mango seed can only give us mango fruits. We reap what we sow. Love is revealed by the fact that a single mango seed does not just give us one mango fruit but many. In fact, a single seed has the potential to yield hundreds of mango trees. Therefore, we not only reap what we sow but also reap it in abundance. We take it for granted that one small seed could yield hundreds of fruits, but upon deeper contemplation, isn't this magical? We put a seed in the ground and in a few months or years, we receive a bounty of nutritious fruits. It is the same with the seeds of our thoughts, words, and actions.

"Try it, for your thoughts are the messengers you send forth, which return *heavily laden* with similar thought-forms, good or evil as the case may be." This quote from *The Grail Message* shared earlier in the chapter emphasizes the point that the fruits of our thoughts return heavily laden with similar thought forms.

We can see this reflected in today's technology. For example, the algorithm of Google's search engine optimization process is based on this principle. It seeks to give us more of what it "thinks" we desire.

Take, for instance, two young men who purchase iPhones and quickly acquaint themselves with Google's search engine.

In their spare time, one of them uses his new phone to follow the lives of friends and celebrities, while the other explores his curiosity about electricity generation.

Recognizing his search patterns, Google presents the first young man with countless links and advertisements about celebrities he follows. He can barely keep up with the new information he receives daily. Every free minute, he consumes the information provided by his new device. He realizes this activity is unhealthy but thinks that he, too, should be entitled to a small vice. *I do not smoke or drink, so what harm is there in surfing the web all day long?* he consoles himself. He meets people like himself who enjoy discussing the lives of others.

The other young man is presented with countless links about the generation of electricity. He learns about sources of energy, turbines, magnets, electrons. "So this is not as complex as I thought," he says, amazed. Every free minute, he reads articles about energy generation and contemplates carrying out experiments of his own. The intensity of his thoughts brings him in contact with people who have similar aspirations.

The first man does not see the plethora of vices that accompany time-wasting. And as he wastes his life, so does he also dawdle away the time graciously afforded him to advance spiritually.

The other young man is ignorant of the many virtues that accompany a steadfast, constructive volition. However, in his respect for the time graciously afforded him, he earns the full measure of help that awaits him in Creation, and a success that he attributes to luck, not spiritual law.

\*\*\*

Just as the Google search engine yields multiple results for a single searched item, so does a single vice or virtue consistently nurtured bring forth more of its kind!

The understanding of this principle should encourage us to sow good seeds. Each of us will receive in abundance what we give through our thoughts, words, and deeds. A man who lovingly cooks a meal for his elderly neighbor will be lifted upwards by the threads of his love. His increased lightness and joy will encourage this man to continue on his current path. The woman who boastfully gives away a million dollars, not out of love for her community but to boost her image, will be bound by the threads of her deceit. An increased feeling of heaviness and emptiness will encourage her to reconsider her current path. A selfish man will eventually find himself in an atmosphere of selfishness much greater than his own, where he will have to endure the experience he once inflicted on others. In this lies not only justice but love. His suffering will help to stir him in a direction that will bring him joy.

The understanding of this principle enables us to see ourselves as we truly are, for our experiences reveal the fruits of our volition. A farmer who plants tomato seeds in the spring and nurtures them through the spring will not be surprised to find tomatoes in his garden in the summer. If he is unsatisfied with tomatoes and prefers cucumbers the following season, he must clear the tomatoes from his garden and prepare the soil to receive cucumber seeds in the spring. If he doubts that the cucumber seeds will germinate and wane in watering the seeds, his doubts will likely be realized in the summer. The same applies to the seeds of our volition.

Each of us is afforded the opportunity to taste the fruits of our inmost desires and decide whether we wish to stay on a chosen path or change course. The fruits sometimes arrive long after we expect them, but they will eventually arrive. If we wish to be happy and successful, we must clear away the seeds of selfishness and indolence and prepare the soil in our hearts to receive happiness and success by serving others cheerfully.

In the late nineteenth century, a teenage artist named Walter Russell took a summer job as a bellboy at a hotel. His wages were eight dollars a month, but he was told that he could earn upwards of one hundred dollars in a season with tips. When he was first offered a tip, something deep within prevented him from accepting it. Caught off guard by the offer, he stammered as he searched for words to excuse himself. He went down to his room in the cellar to ponder why he had just turned down much-needed income. Suddenly, he felt an inner lightness that confirmed the rightness of his decision. He resolved to be the only bellboy who never took a tip and to be the best bellboy the world ever knew. He pledged himself to give the most cheerful service. He got up at five o'clock in the morning and ran his legs off for every guest he served. Whenever he was asked why he did not accept tips, he replied, "I receive a salary, and I love my work." This endeared him to his guests who had never seen anyone like him. They invited him to dinner parties and yachting trips. On one occasion, the hotel manager explained that it was against hotel policy for servants to have social relations with guests, and the wealthy guest said they would not return to the hotel if an exception was not made. The hotel management made the exception, and the young artist had a great summer.

The wealthy guests took to Russell's artwork and bought some of his sketches and paintings. Instead of the one hundred dollars he was told he could have received from tips, he received checks amounting to eight hundred and fifty dollars for his artwork. He received many future commissions for painting from the friends he made at the hotel. From his experience that summer, the young artist learned a valuable life lesson—good things come to a person who gives more to others than they expect and does so cheerfully.

***

If we find ourselves surrounded by fruits of unhappiness, the power to plant a different seed is at our disposal.

# Justice returns to us what we give, and love multiplies it.

The love spoken of here is not the weak, all-forgiving, sentimental thing we call love on earth. Like the sun, Divine love is giving, impartial, and impersonal. It seeks the long-term interests of the loved one, and not what pleases that person in the short term. If a person wishes to forge ahead on a road that will bring him inner suffering, that is his choice. He will not, however, be spared the difficulties that await him on his chosen path. He will be forced to learn that his chosen path is not the right path for him.

Love and justice cannot be separated, for they are interlinked. There is no justice without love and no love without justice. A justice that seeks to punish out of hatred is not justice but revenge. Justice does not punish out of wickedness. It places us in the environment where we can experience the fruits of our thoughts and actions. It *lovingly* holds up a mirror so that we see ourselves as we truly are. The love and justice of the Creator ultimately lead us to freedom and joy if we learn to see it amid our daily experiences. Creation speaks to us through our experiences, through our intuition, and through our environment. Just as a child must first learn the language of his parents if he wishes to be happy, so must we learn the language of Creation.

## A Glimpse into the Nature of The Creator

How can we gain insight into the nature of the Creator if we have no physical access to Him? The same way we would proceed if we were seeking to discover the nature of a distant earthly king. By observing the spirit of the king's laws and their impact on the daily lives of citizens. Through this observation, the Creator's sublimity, perfection, mercy, patience, love, and justice is revealed.

*Sublimity* – An observation of any of the celestial bodies surrounding us—such as the sun, moon, and stars—gives evidence of their Creator's sublime nature.

*Perfection* – The interconnectedness of all things in Nature displays the wisdom and perfection of its designer. Look no further than your body. See how each organ works together with the others in the maintenance of the body.

*Mercy and Patience* – The sun shines on all. We are not cast out when we make mistakes but are given several opportunities to mature through our experiences.

*Love and Justice* – Justice gives to each his due. Love multiplies it. We always reap what we sow; hence, every effect has a cause. "Our inability to see the connection between cause and effect merely proves the inadequacy of our ability to judge and not the absence of justice." (Dr. Richard Steinpach)

*The Little Things in Action:*

For two minutes every night this week, look up at the night sky and just allow your mind to wander.

# Part II

# OUR TRUE PURPOSE IN LIFE

The wisdom of the Creator rules the universe. The observation of our natural surroundings as well as the laws of Nature provide a glimpse into His sublime nature. His perfection, mercy, patience, love, and justice are observable if we wish to see it.

Let us now turn our attention to humankind.

How do we fit into the Creator's great design? Why are we on earth? Is there life after death? How do we find Truth? Where do we go after death? We will explore these questions in this section.

CHAPTER 5

# **Why Are We on Earth?**

> You do not live in order to have an easy life, as you
> long to. You live in order to experience! Learn from
> your failures, learn from your good fortune. Look
> around you; you are not on the earth to disregard it.
> — *Unknown*

In one of my favorite scenes in the film *Gladiator*, Emperor
Marcus Aurelius knows he doesn't have much time left on
earth due to his failing health. So he selects his most loyal
soldier, Maximus, as his heir instead of his immoral son,
Commodus. In this scene, the emperor says to the soldier,
"Tell me again, Maximus, why are we here? . . . I am dying,
Maximus. When a man sees his end, he wants to know there
was some purpose to his life."

What is the purpose of our lives? I am sure that most of
us have asked ourselves this question at some point. Some
people think so much about it that it becomes a draining
intellectual exercise, while others give it little thought. We
need neither rack our brains too much about this question

nor fearfully silence the inner voice that periodically draws our attention to it.

In the following story, let's turn to Nature, once again, for clues that might shed light on the answer to this question.

In a small village, a young farmer was lost in thought as he watered his crops. He could not understand why children were born into this world of trials if heaven was immensely more beautiful and peaceful.

"Why leave heaven for earth?" he quietly asked.

While planting green peppers the following day, a picture suddenly arose within him.

He paused . . . and then voiced a question: "Could being born on earth be likened to a seed being planted in the soil?"

The farmer pondered this question. From one seed, he could potentially grow many crops to sell at the local market. But this potential cannot be realized until the seed journeys down beneath the soil. It needs this period of struggle in search of nutrients from the soil to develop its innate qualities, after which it rises as a plant bearing rich fruits and enriches his farm.

*Perhaps the same applies to human beings,* he thought, *starting as a seed with bountiful potential in heaven that needs to extract the appropriate nutrients from its experiences on earth in order to develop its innate qualities.* After which it rises from the earth as a spiritually matured human spirit able to contribute actively to the joyful activities of heaven.

"*It must be so,*" said the young farmer. He smiled at the simplicity of it all and was thankful for his new insight.

***

Just as the oak tree sleeps in the acorn so does the noble human spirit lie within its outer shell waiting to become all that it was meant to be. The joys and sorrows, the sunny and rainy days, the successes and failures of life—all of this orients us toward spiritual growth. The tangible results of our efforts are not nearly as important as the habits and character we develop in the struggle for the achievements pursued. The achievements will remain behind, but the habits we developed in our earthy pursuits will long outlast the physical body and pave our path in the beyond.

Deep within us lies an inner guidance that sometimes urges us to reach for our higher selves.

In quiet moments, we feel there must be more to life than satisfying our physiological and social needs.

The search for Truth drives us to reassess what we hold on to as Truth. The desire to know the rights and responsibilities of a human spirit according to the Creator's design must awaken in us. For how else can we fulfill our purpose and be free? Opportunities to know these rights and responsibilities are provided to us, but we seem to be too busy to listen. Even in the occasion when we have some respite from our daily responsibilities, something else swoops in to take up precious time that could have helped us find our true path.

Take, for instance, time-saving inventions from the past century such as vacuum cleaners, refrigerators, and washing machines that enable us to complete monotonous tasks in a fraction of the time they would otherwise take. The time we save could give us more opportunities for inner reflection and engagement in meaningful work. Today's consumer electronics perform tasks that would have been unimaginable to most just two decades ago. But do we find more time for inner reflection and meaningful work? Or are we busier than ever? A life filled with work but without any spiritual aim is like a peach that looks ripe on the outside but whose fruit remains unripe within. The physical body may be active and keeping pace with Nature's rhythm of movement, but the spirit within stands still. Without the inner movement of the spirit, we lack spiritual inspiration, and our body will become exhausted by its work rather than being strengthened by it.

For a long time now, we have felt obliged to *busy* ourselves with the illusion that we are productive members of society, while in reality, we are running away from the actual work that is ourselves. We may try to numb this inner longing for Truth by diverting our attention outward to the accumulation of earthly treasures, through the rush of work, or even self-medicating, but we cannot escape the reality of our spiritual origin. The unavoidable search for Truth must commence if we wish for inner peace.

Everyone knows that death approaches us closer with each passing day, yet for most people, there is little urgency to achieve the highest goal of life. We attend the funeral of a neighbor but hardly imagine our time too will come. Why not give death the respect it deserves by seeking the meaning of life? If we do, we may discover that death is not so terrible after all.

> "If you do not take death seriously, life
> will plunge you into seriousness.
>
> But if you live with death in mind, life
> will not be able to harm you.
>
> With death in mind and that which follows it,
>
> You will stride through life as one who
> lives it and feels not its severity."

These ancient words, attributed to a Chinese sage long before the time of Lao-Tzu, convey great wisdom. Ask your closest friends why they are on earth, and you will quickly realize how little thought is given to this topic. When people do not know why they live, they are easily susceptible to the traps of persuasive men and women who seek personal glory at their expense. History gives ample evidence of this fact.

Those who have considered this question may say they live for their family; others may say they live for their profession or calling. Upon further reflection, you may realize that family and work are tools that aid our spiritual development. Consider this idea: could it be that we live for the sake of developing spiritually through these activities— and not for the activities themselves?

"If you do not take death seriously, life will plunge you into seriousness. But if you live with death in mind, life will not be able to harm you." What does this mean?

Let us picture a literature student at the university who just received her final grade for her chemistry class. She failed! If she has no vision of life beyond the classroom, and no vision of a goal, such as to become a writer or teacher, she will be devastated. But if she lives with a vision of life beyond the classroom, she will be more concerned about taking the lessons from the failed class that will help her in her quest to become a writer or whatever she chooses to be. It is no different with the struggles and calamities of life. These things become less severe and cannot seriously harm those who live with death in mind and that which follows it. Observation of life reveals that we are only temporary custodians of our bodies and possessions; we own nothing. Our bodies, possessions, family, and friends are all temporary—we leave it all behind. All we take with us are the experiences of the spirit.

## Therefore, we are on earth to develop spiritually through our experiences.

This development will ultimately lead to our greatest happiness.

# Chapter 6

# Is There Life After Death?

For life and death are one, even as the
rivers and the sea are one
— *Khalil Gibran*

Those who question the existence of life beyond the grave are well within their right to question it. If we are earnest in our questioning, however, we will surely find the answer. For instance, perhaps a man could gain insight from seeing a pregnant woman sitting opposite him on the train. Picture him striking up a conversation with this young woman and learning that she is expecting twin boys. Upon leaving the train, his thoughts remain with the pregnant woman, and he imagines what life must be like for the twins in the womb:

In the belly of this pregnant woman were twin brothers, Leo and Tao, in conversation.

Leo: "Do you believe in life after birth?"

Tao: "Yes, I picture us running free on our two feet and eating with our mouths."

Leo: "Run on our two feet? Eat with our mouths? How is this possible?"

Tao: "There must be some bigger world out there. I feel it. I just cannot explain it."

Leo: "This is foolishness. If we leave here that's the end of us."

Tao: "Don't you think there is someone out there who will take care of us after birth?

Doesn't that prove that there is life after birth?"

Leo: "Do you see anyone? It is just you and me here."

Tao: "When we are silent, I sometimes hear a voice singing and feel someone stroking us in our world. I believe this person takes care of us now and will continue to do so when we leave here."

Leo: "That is true. I sometimes hear faint singing, but I cannot be sure it means there is life outside here. No one has ever come back from birth to verify the existence of life after birth."

This scene may seem silly to you, but is the question of whether there is life after birth essentially any different from asking whether there is life after death? Just as the fetus dwells in its mother's womb, so do we currently dwell in a womb called earth. Just as a mother sustains the growing child in her womb, so does the power of the Creator sustain our life on the earth. The twins in their mother's womb would hardly imagine the greater world awaiting them outside the womb. They can hardly imagine the abilities of their physical bodies that they are yet to fully develop and all the good things they can achieve. The same applies to us as we strut about in the limited space of earth, unaware of the abilities of the spirit that we are yet to develop fully. The answers to the great questions of life need not be a mystery; they often lie amid our everyday experiences. As in little things on earth, so it is in the great world of spiritual events.

While on a trip to Austria, I met a talented pianist who occasionally hears music from some unknown world. In these instances, he immediately runs to the nearest piano to materialize the sound, which is as real to him as if he had heard it on the radio. He plays the song a few times and remembers it without having to write it down. He had no formal training in music and did not even know how to read music. His gift is his ability to share with us on earth beautiful sounds he receives from a world unknown to us.

We may not hear beautiful music from the beyond during our waking hours, but we all dream at night. You might be familiar with REM (rapid eye movement) and non-REM sleep cycles. During REM sleep, which can be measured by an oculometer, the eyes move rapidly in various directions behind the lids and don't send any visual information to the brain. It is during this period that we have deep dreams. Aren't there times you have dreams that are so vivid they don't feel like dreams at all but actual experiences of the spirit in some place beyond the earth?

In astronomy, the geocentric model sees the earth as the center of the universe with the sun and the other celestial bodies moving around the earth. This was the predominant description of the cosmos for several centuries in various ancient European civilizations. Imagine the absurdity of tiny earth, unrecognizable among the billions of stars in our galaxy, being the center of the universe. Although we know better today, we still make the same mistake when we harbor the mindset that sees our current existence on earth as the center of our entire existence. With this mindset, we narrow our ability to see the bigger picture. Our time on earth is only a short period of our entire existence. If this were not the case, what could possibly be the purpose of our brief time on earth? For example, what would be the point of college if nothing existed beyond college graduation? What would be the point of our earthly lives if nothing existed beyond our earthly deaths?

Earlier, in the chapter about justice in Part 1, we mentioned that everything seen physically is the result of an unseen process. We see evidence of this all around us. For example, what is the difference between a leaf still connected by the stem to the branch of a tree and one that has just fallen to the ground? What is the difference between a strand of human hair that is still connected to the body and one that fell off in the shower? Our physical eyes see no difference, but there is a great difference between them. Both the leaf on the ground and the strand of hair on the shower floor can no longer grow. Something that we can't see with our physical eyes, even by looking with the most powerful microscope, is missing. This "something" is essential for the growth of the leaf and the strand of hair. Now, let's take this further. What is the difference between a human body that is alive and one that is dead? Something that was previously in the body and kept it alive must have left it, right? What is it exactly that keeps the blood flowing through the body? Can any instrument on earth see it? Where does this "something" go after it leaves the body? We will address this in a later chapter.

To question things is not only healthy but it should be encouraged. That is why we are given the ability to think. We will find answers to the mysteries of life if we do not close ourselves to this understanding through our prejudice. For those who still seek scientific proof of the continuation of life beyond the grave, know that the brain from which scientific proof is obtained is too limited to grasp concepts beyond the material world. The analytical mind cannot possibly comprehend, let alone render judgment on, anything beyond the limits of its origin in the material world. Our material senses are so inadequate that they cannot even perceive the infrared light waves used by a remote control to change the television channel. The attitude of regarding everything invisible as "unnatural" clips the wings of our spirit. Only the spirit has access to higher knowledge. The more spiritually alive we become, the more our awareness of the eternal Truths of life naturally expands.

The understanding that we are on earth to develop spiritually in preparation for life beyond the earth is important. But how do we proceed on this path of spiritual development?

CHAPTER 7

# How Do We Find Truth?

Knowledge can be conveyed but not wisdom. It cannot
be expressed in word and thought. Wisdom which a
wise man tries to pass on to someone always sounds
like foolishness
— *Herman Hesse*

Abraham Lincoln is credited with saying that if he had an hour to chop down a tree, he would spend the first forty-five minutes sharpening his axe. This is a popular quote used to convey the importance of thoughtfulness and calmness before action. In the eagerness to begin, we sometimes omit important steps and doom the task to failure from the onset. The quality of the tool used makes a big difference in the performance of a task. A dull axe would make the work very difficult, if not impossible.

Before embarking on an important task, it is wise to develop the abilities and tools needed to accomplish it. The search for Truth is no different. Truth is eternal and thus cannot be truly grasped by our earthly senses which are incapable of penetrating the realms beyond the material world.

# Our intuition is the avenue through which the highest wisdom is revealed to us.

It is the tool that will help us find the path to Truth. We sharpen this tool through our honest and earnest striving for the highest ideals within us. This striving opens us more and more to the spiritual currents from above. We become more accustomed to the way of Truth and can more easily recognize all things connected with Truth. The decision not to settle for mediocrity but to awaken the best and highest within us is the first step on the path to Truth. The following story about a young man's quest for the highest ideals within him portrays the value of the sage advice "Seek and ye shall find."

The beloved Marza was the delight of his parents. The handsome, bright eighteen-year-old had long since joined the council of wise men, for they all saw in him their future chief priest and king.

Marza's regal gait, radiant smile, and piercing dark eyes conveyed strength to the onlooker. He brought joy to all. And yet his own heart was bereft of joy. Strolling in the woods one day, troubling thoughts assailed him. The love of the villagers and the praise and reverence he received at every turn burdened him. *There must be something more*, he thought. He sensed it.

To the great sadness of his parents and the people of his village, Marza resolved to chart his course in search of that something more. Something that would satisfy the intense inner longing that gave him no peace. He joined a nomadic monastic group, subjugating himself to the privations and discipline of the group, but he soon realized that they could not give him what he sought.

The young man went off on his own and traveled for a few years until he came to a small town where he had heard there lived a great master. He was skeptical, for he had begun to doubt the effectiveness of teachings and gurus. Nonetheless, he journeyed to find this master, and the instant he saw him, Marza knew that this master possessed what he had sought. Every movement of the master revealed his nobility of soul. To Marza, it was as if the master were one with the eternal powers of Creation.

He listened with his whole being as this great master addressed a crowd outside in the open. With eyes closed, the master faced upwards toward the sun, as if to drink of its radiance. Right there and then, Marza too felt a connection with the eternal powers. He was overcome by a wave of victorious strength and calmness. He had found what he had been searching for!

His earnest longing for the highest had led him to the great master whose presence opened the treasure chest in his spirit. Filled with this newfound wealth, Marza dropped to his knees in gratitude. "So I possessed this all along," the young man stammered. Only now did he understand why the teachings he was previously exposed to had fallen short of his expectations. He had possessed an inner awareness of the highest; it only needed to be awakened by the great master's Word. Victorious in his quest, Marza happily began the long journey back to his village. He would share with his people the truth he had discovered in his years of traveling.

The truth that within each of us lies the true teacher. The truth that there can be no greater authority than the spark of light within. Therefore, we do ourselves a disservice when we abandon our inner guidance in favor of the opinion of others. And most importantly, the truth that our earnest longing for the highest is what brings us to the presence of the great master's Word. For it is only His Word that can give us the knowledge we need to awaken and develop the spark of light within.

*\*\**

Making a serious decision to search sets events in motion that will lead to finding that which we seek. We then see our environment with new eyes, and as a result, gain useful recognitions from our experiences. The process is the same, whether we make a serious decision to search for the light of truth or decide to search for earthly knowledge with the goal of becoming a medical doctor, for example. The course of study alone is not sufficient to gain this medical knowledge. The information must be applied. The topics covered in the classroom come to life only when we see and experience them in real life. Every medical student must pass through residency or some sort of practical training before a medical degree is earned. The same principle applies to spiritual knowledge. The study of spiritual texts alone is not sufficient. We must bring them to life in our daily experiences. Regardless of the object of our innermost desire, this principle applies.

Once we make the
earnest decision to
attain what we desire,
we will be led to where
we can find it.

We then begin noticing what we seek all around us.

While I was preparing for a trip from Boston,
Massachusetts, to Lagos, Nigeria, I had a friend ask me
to buy her a handbag. She sent me samples of the type of
handbags she liked. With the samples in mind, I went to
the mall but could not find any exactly like the samples she
sent me. Returning home, I browsed online hoping to find
the exact type she desired. I found one that was close, but I
knew she wouldn't like the color.

With my trip fast approaching, I intensified my efforts
and decided to visit a different store after work. While on
the train on my way to work, I found myself, for the first
time in my life, paying attention to the different handbags
on women's arms. Sometimes approving the quality and

design, and other times critiquing the handbag choice. I had to laugh. Since when did I become so interested in women's handbags?

I thought about this question and realized that it was only after my search for a handbag that I began noticing them all around me. It dawned on me that the nature of our earnest desire determines how we will see and hear the things before us. Our strongest desire at any particular moment determines what we see and what we fail to notice. As with my experience with the handbag, so it is with the search for Truth. We will notice the eternal Truth of life all around us. The prerequisite for this higher awareness is the earnest desire to find Truth.

To find Truth, we must first find the path that leads to Truth. I wish to assure you that this path to Truth is not a mystical concept but a very real and practical thing. We must heed the inner guidance that urges us to reach for our higher selves. This is so important. Never settle for average for there is no such thing as average in the ever-active machinery of Creation. There are only two categories: useful and useless. Only by developing our abilities can we keep pace with the rhythm of Creation and thereby become useful. On this journey toward spiritual maturity, we will make mistakes, but we should not for that reason settle for mediocrity. Despite our setbacks, we can correct the errors of the past and get back on the path to Truth. We have family and financial obligations, career and personal aspirations—challenges coming at us from every direction. How can the search for the path to Truth be the predominant desire amid all the struggles of life?

In my mid-twenties, I met a young man of similar age. Ben was his name. He was paid well and lived in a nice apartment in Boston. He was a frugal man with modest needs who took public transportation, brought his lunch to work, and had little interest in the expensive nightlife of his lively city. Beyond his occasional travels, he spent little money outside of his living expenses. Ben saved whatever money was left over every month but had no definite financial goal. He met a girl who multiplied the joy in his life and would later become his wife. But even after marrying his bride, his pattern remained unchanged.

With each passing year, however, his desire for financial security and a home to shelter his young family grew stronger until it became a goal. Ben no longer merely saved what was left over from every paycheck; rather, he first allocated funds toward this objective. With his goal clearly before him, he became attuned to all the opportunities around him that served the attainment of his goal, and he realized it much sooner than he ever imagined possible.

*\*\**

As it is in our earthly pursuits, so it is with spiritual aspirations. There will be all kinds of distractions until we realize that most things are not truly essential. Yet we invest much of our time on the non-essentials while ignoring the few essential things. Identify and invest in the essential first, and all else will take care of itself. Only when we see a goal clearly before us and take little steps daily toward the goal do we begin to live with purpose.

Our highest goal determines all things because all things will be seen from the perspective of this goal. It is important to know that we are here on earth to develop spiritually. But how do we develop spiritually?

Take the example of a middle-aged woman named Jasmine who renews her commitment to the gym after a dozen years of absence. She feels pain and soreness all over her body after her first week of workouts. She feels like quitting. Formerly, she did not experience soreness all over her body, nor did she have this much difficulty breathing. Jasmine is tempted to give up this dream of improving her health and revert to her more comfortable lifestyle without the painful exertions at the gym. Her friends would be happy to have her back, for they miss her company. They themselves are overweight and don't understand Jasmine's sudden resolve to get in shape.

Over the past twelve years, Jasmine did not prioritize her health, and the cumulative effect of her neglect has brought her to this point. If she will persevere a few more weeks with the workouts, the soreness and pain will certainly subside and the improved health she seeks will be hers.

Jasmine's fitness challenge is a little like when a malevolent foreign power invades a country. The pain of fighting back will be much greater than surrendering in the short term; but by surrendering, they will be forever subservient to the foreign power.

Jasmine does not give up. She keeps at it. As a result, her disciplined commitment to the gym not only improves her physical health, but she also sees benefits in every aspect of her life because of her increased self-confidence. A major part of self-confidence stems from not neglecting to do the small, daily disciplines. We all feel good about ourselves when we put forth our best each day. Stack up a few weeks of doing these daily disciplines, and self-confidence expands. Ignore the daily disciplines and self-confidence shrinks.

It is no different with spiritual perspiration. We must first find the courage to honestly look within to see ourselves as we are now, not as we aspire to be. And then find the humility to seek to improve ourselves without blaming anything or anybody else. The strength to replace bad habits with good ones will naturally follow. These things are simple but not easy to do. We may fail many times, but we cannot give up. With every temporary defeat, we are gifted with permanent pearls of wisdom if we take the time to find them.

For example, a mentor whom you hold in high regard may grossly disappoint you. Remember to give your allegiance to the Creator, not to any human being. This will save you much heartache. The hypocrisy of a guardian or mentor has caused many people to give up their search for Truth entirely. But your spiritual development is too important to be dependent on a human being. It is a personal journey between you and your Creator. There is no other favorable alternative than to keep climbing, to keep honestly striving.

In your increasing search for the light of truth, you may find yourself alone. But do not lose heart. Your friends and family may not understand your questions. Just keep asking. Your community may abandon you if you share your increasing light, but just keep shining. The light exposes the filth amid the darkness. It is welcoming to those who wish to free themselves of filth, but dreadful to those who are comfortable under the cover of darkness. Do not give up! Exercise your spiritual muscles daily by dwelling in the wisdom of spiritual texts and engaging in activities that awaken the highest within you.

# Spend less time admiring the beauty of others and more time developing your own.

The help of the Creator surrounds us and will see us through any difficulty... if we do not abandon the high ideals within us.

# CHAPTER 8

# How Do We Transform Recognition into Action?

The End Of All Knowledge Should
Be Service To God

On the path of our spiritual development, certain responsibilities are given to us. Good parents develop their children by giving them responsibilities and holding them accountable for their actions. In the same manner, the path to spiritual maturity lies in the fulfillment of responsibilities. It is our responsibility to learn the Will of the Creator and transform the earth into a paradise. But we can only fulfill this task by knowing the tools we possess and understanding our place in the larger context of Creation. Our search for Truth alone is not sufficient for spiritual transformation. The insights we gain must be applied and transformed into actions that lead to the ennoblement of the earth and all creatures in it. Take the following example of the impact of Colonel Anderson's simple act of kindness on the young boys of Allegheny.

In the mid-1800s, Colonel James Anderson decided to open his library of over three hundred books to the young working boys in the town of Allegheny, Pennsylvania. These were mostly teenage boys who worked eight to twelve hours a day to support their families, boys who would not otherwise have been able to afford the books in Colonel Anderson's library.

The impact of Colonel Anderson's simple kindness was life-changing. In the words of one of those boys:

> "My dear friend, Tom Miller, one of the inner circle, lived near Colonel Anderson and introduced me to him, and in this way the windows were opened in the walls of my dungeon through which the light of knowledge streamed in. Every day's toil and even the long hours of night service were lightened by the book which I carried about with me and read in the intervals that could be snatched from duty. And the future was made bright by the thought that when Saturday came a new volume could be obtained. . . . Nothing contributed so much to keep my companions and myself clear of low fellowship and bad habits as the beneficence of the good Colonel."

This boy was Andrew Carnegie. He would grow up to be a steel tycoon and repay the good colonel's kindness tenfold by using his massive fortune to support educational institutions and build thousands of libraries around the world as well as theaters and child welfare centers.

Regardless of our circumstances, we all have the ability to shine our light wide and make our communities more prosperous and beautiful. Colonel Anderson gave what he most treasured: his love for books. What is it that you wish to give? Countless are the opportunities offered daily to serve others. A simple act of kindness rooted in love for the well-being of another is the starting point. The great ability at our disposal is our free will to decide. Through our thoughts, words, and actions, we have the power to further the spread of light or further the spread of darkness. As illustrated earlier with the Google search example, each decision has a multiplying effect. The decision to direct our thoughts and deeds to the highest ideals or relegate ourselves to mediocrity is the choice of every human being. We often complain that we don't have enough time or enough money. Don't ask for more time without first putting to productive use the free time you already have. Don't ask for more money without first wisely deploying the little money at your disposal. Don't expect changes in your environment or your relationships without first changing yourself within. Simply begin with the *decision* to love more.

Melina's mother's fiftieth birthday was fast approaching, but Melina had no idea what to get her for a gift. She called her big sister, Suyapa, for guidance.

"Mom enjoys singing, so why not get her a one-year membership to the Tewksbury Chorus group?" Suyapa suggested. "It will encourage her to improve her singing, and it is quite close to the house."

"Yes! That is a great idea. You always have the best gift ideas," Melina happily exclaimed.

She thanked her sister and hung up the phone. Suddenly, she was overcome by a question. *How does Suyapa do this? How does she always know what people need?* Just two weeks ago, she had received a pair of thermal underwear from Suyapa, which was exactly what she needed to protect herself against the harsh Toronto winter. After musing on this question for a few minutes, the answer unexpectedly dawned on her. *She loves more; therefore, she sees more.*

She recalled how attentive Suyapa always was during their conversations. How her questions in one way or another sought to find out the true state of her spirit, to find out how she really was, and to offer the encouragement Melina needed. It became abundantly clear to Melina that her sister knew what people needed because she cared about them. It was that simple.

Smiling, she felt gratitude for her dear sister and strove to follow her example. She soon found herself constantly occupied with the question "How can I serve?" And a new world opened to her. For the first time, she could see the lonely eyes of her neighbor whom she had always greeted superficially. Where she formerly just concerned herself with her own job at work, she now saw its connection to the whole organization. In her loving attentiveness within her circle of friends, she now heard what their words sometimes failed to express, and consequently, she could be a better friend.

# The currency of the universe is love, and it is free for all to amass in great quantity.

Every creature gains its respect and worth by its usefulness to the whole. Love is the greatest power there is because the Creator Himself is love. Our connection to Him is strongest when our actions are guided by love. The question for each human being then becomes, *How great is my love?* Love is the engine that enables us to transform our spiritual recognitions into action.

CHAPTER 9

# What Determines Where We Go After Death?

Don't depend on death to liberate you from your
imperfections. You are exactly the same after death as you
were before. Nothing changes; you only give up the body
— *Paramahansa Yogananda*

There are differing opinions about what awaits us after
death, but the fundamental idea is quite simple. The nature
of our thoughts determines where we go after death. For
several years, I took the train to work and was fascinated
by the intricate railway network with all its intersecting
routes. There were many trains at the train station, each
going to a different destination. The only determining
factor that influenced the choice of train for each person
was the volition of the individual. Some were going home
after working the night shift, others were going to daycare
to drop off their children, some were going to school, and
others were going to work. Each is driven by their
desire which determines the appropriate train that will
get them to their desired destination. All we do is pick

our train of choice; the power driving the train does the rest. As it is with the choice of trains, so it is with our choice of thoughts. All we do is decide the nature of our thoughts; the power that drives Creation does the rest. We want to get to paradise but often harbor thoughts that lead us in the opposite direction. Where we go after death is dependent on our innermost desires. Picture the following story:

Perplexed, a young man finds himself sitting alone in the front seat of a rapidly moving car. What is propelling this vehicle, and where is it heading? He knows not. The car takes him through ugly towns and cities. On rare occasions, the vehicle shifts direction, and he rides through the beautiful countryside. "Why this darkness, why this ugliness? Go back to the beautiful countryside," he yells at the car. He yells louder but to no avail. How much longer would this last? Hopeless, he surrenders to his fate. The monotonous gloominess, which felt as if it had lasted for years, became too much for the poor man to bear. Helpless and filled with fear, he cried out for help.

His humble petition was soon rewarded. The car slowed down and turned toward the beautiful countryside. The sight of the sun and the magnificent mountains filled him with such deep gratitude. With tears coursing down his cheeks, he thanked the car. He thanked the Creator of the sun and the mountains. In his state of joy and gratitude, he wished to admire the beautiful flowers in the meadow. To his surprise, the car obeyed this silent volition and drove him closer to the flowers. He wished to see the flowing stream, and again the vehicle obeyed his unspoken desire and drove him closer to the stream. "For years I saw mostly darkness, ugliness, and filth. Why didn't you grant my wish to see the countryside then? Why do you only listen to me now?" lamented the young man.

He thought about this for a while and soon discovered the difference between his outward wishes and his innermost desire. He now knew that the vehicle had always listened to him, for it was propelled by his desire. It could not obey his wish to go to the beautiful countryside because his innermost desire was primarily filled with dark aspirations that drew him to the ugly towns and cities.

The power bestowed upon him to direct his destiny through his free will became clear to him. Shaking, he trembled at the greatness of this recognition and gave thanks for it.

*** 

Whether we can see it or not, we are where we are because of our innermost desires. Our innermost desires will also determine where we find ourselves after leaving behind the physical body. Everything seen externally is the result of an inward process. As with the perplexed young man, we must learn to distinguish between our outward wishes and our innermost desires. How can we do this?

What activities do you gravitate toward the moment you have some free time? Is there a constructive goal you are working toward, or do you constantly find yourself aimlessly browsing the internet? The answer to this question will provide great insight into the nature of your innermost desires. Observe your habits in daily life and honestly ask yourself what value it brings. Where is it taking you? You cannot expect to get to the beautiful countryside while engaged in habits that do not inspire beauty. Observe your state of being after watching a particular television program or listening to a certain song. Do you feel uplifted? Observe your manner of speech and dress. Does it give evidence of refinement of spirit and nobility of soul?

It is important to remember that we have the free will to decide between light and darkness. Between the beautiful countryside and the ugly town. The Creator's help is available to us, but we must prepare within ourselves the fertile soil that can receive this help. Trust in Him is essential, as is our trust in the abilities He has given us. Chief among these is the ability to think and decide—our free will. We must use this ability consciously; otherwise, we become powerless and will be influenced by the agenda of others. By purposefully using our free will, we will create works that beautify our surroundings and thereby pave our way to the beautiful realms above after our time on earth expires.

In 1822, Louis Schlösser visited Ludwig van Beethoven and asked the composer how he goes about his work. The maestro responded as follows:

"I carry my thoughts about me for a long time,

sometimes a very long time, before I set them down. . . . I make many changes, reject and reattempt until I am satisfied. . . . I am conscious of what I want, the basic idea never leaves me. It rises, grows upward, and I hear and see the picture as a whole take shape and stand forth before me as though cast in a single piece, so that all is left is the work of writing it down."

Inspiration follows aspiration. Noble aspirations nurtured over time will rise and garner support from the higher realms. The association with the higher realms transforms and refines our initial noble volition, thus bringing about a more perfect idea, work, or an expanded state of inner peace. We have all experienced this at some point. How many times have you thought about something deeply and later received a solution that you cannot possibly attribute to your knowledge? Where do you think the idea came from?

Confused or distracted thoughts, on the other hand, can only produce mediocre works at best. Beethoven's experience is not unique. It is the same with all men and women of history who have produced creative works that stood the test of time. It is the same with you and me. One who understands this would strive to insulate their mind from all distractions that dissipate their energy and divert them away from their intended purpose. Alexander Graham Bell, the inventor of the telephone, understood this quite well, which is why he once said to author Orison Swett Marden, in response to his question whether hard study was necessary for success, "Concentrate all your thoughts upon the work at hand. The sun's rays do not burn until brought to a focus." Just as thieves will rob a wealthy man who continually leaves his house unlocked, so will our fluctuating desires and impulses rob us of the strength needed for the pursuit of our earnest aspirations if we continually leave the gate to our thoughts wide open.

We are influenced by the content we consistently consume, whether from television, social media, music, books, or friends. Not to think so is naïve. If we do not consciously decide what we want for ourselves, we will receive what others want to give us. Is there a bigger slave than one who thinks he is free without being free? What, then, does it mean to be free?

A six-year-old girl whose only wish is to bring joy to her parents and have fun with her friends is free. She understands the expectations of her parents and fulfills her responsibilities. She harbors no ill will toward anyone and has no reason to fear any repercussions. Similarly, if we wish to be free, knowledge of the abilities we possess as human spirits and the responsibility we bear is essential. We have a responsibility to ennoble our environment through our thoughts, words, and deeds. Our task is to transform the earth into a paradise by first transforming ourselves. When we are engaged in this task, we are on the path to real freedom and have nothing to fear.

Whether we like it or not, we are being driven by an unseen power. We steer this power with our volition—our thoughts. By the nature of our thoughts, we decide the direction in which the power will drive us, whether to the beautiful countryside or the ugly town.

# As birds of a feather flock together on earth, so do men and women of similar desires move together in the beyond.

Earlier in the book, we discussed how justice places us in the exact environment that is most conducive to our spiritual development. We discussed the example of how a selfish man will eventually find himself in the company of others who are more selfish than him, thereby forcing him to experience what he once inflicted on others. He will be forced to eat the bitter fruits he once sowed so that he learns to rid himself of selfishness. Those with noble aspirations will find themselves in the company of noble people in beautiful realms. Those with dark aspirations will find themselves in the company of others with similar aspirations in dark realms. The earth is unique in that it allows people with all kinds of aspirations to live side by side. This is not the case in the beyond. Once the physical body is discarded after earthly death, each spirit is drawn to its homogeneous environment.

The earth is like a training ground where we are exposed to all kinds of people and intense conditions to help us expedite our spiritual maturity. Therefore, each day on earth is a blessing because it gives us the opportunity to purify our spirits. In the beyond, we will be among homogeneous spirits. Those striving for paradise will dwell together with their kind undisturbed by human spirits without high spiritual goals. Likewise, those without high spiritual goals will dwell together with their kind, and without the positive influence of more spiritually mature human spirits as they had while on earth. Therefore, we ought to make haste to be among those earnestly striving for paradise before our time on earth comes to an end. The understanding of our responsibility along with an increasing awareness of the power of our volition is of utmost importance. This understanding will shape the formation of positive new habits that lead to the ennoblement of Creation. Before engaging in an activity, ask yourself, What value will this bring? Where will this take me?

As with our life on earth, the realm where we find ourselves immediately after earthly death is not a final destination but a temporary one. We will keep developing either upwards to our spiritual home or downwards to darkness. A more detailed explanation is available should you earnestly desire to have this knowledge. In this book, we will only concern ourselves with the general outline. Once again, where we go after death is formed by our thoughts. Just as you could build a mansion by the ocean if you had the material means, so do we build our homes in the beyond every day with the spiritual power that flows through us every second. We channel this spiritual power with our thoughts. Do you now see why it's so important to think good thoughts and speak words that encourage the spread of beauty and harmony? With each thought we think and with each word we speak, we determine where our path leads after we leave the earth. Will it be to the beautiful countryside or the ugly town?

REFLECTIONS FOR PART II
## Our True Purpose in Life

In quiet moments, we feel there must be more to life than satisfying our physiological and social needs. Certain life questions arise prompting us to search for answers. Where do we find answers to these questions if not from observing our daily experiences?

*Why Are We on Earth?* As a seed journeys beneath the soil to develop its innate qualities after which it rises as a plant bearing rich fruits, so do we descend to the earth to develop our innate spiritual abilities through our experiences on earth.

*Is There Life After Death?* This question is no different from asking if there is life after birth. Just as a fetus dwells in its mother's womb, so do we currently dwell within the earth.

*How Do We Find Truth?* As with any search, the quality of the tool used for the search is of great importance. Our intuition is the avenue through which the highest wisdom is revealed to us. We sharpen this tool by earnestly striving for the highest ideals within us.

*How Do We Transform Recognition into Action?* The search for Truth is not sufficient; we must transform our recognition into action through service. The greater our love, the greater becomes our capacity to see how and where we can serve our communities.

*What Determines Where We Go After Death?* We are where we are because of our innermost desires. Our innermost desires will also determine where we find ourselves after death.

*The Little Things in Action:*

If you had all the required resources at your disposal, what constructive work would you direct your energy towards? Write this down. Also, write down one thing you can do today to move closer to this line of work.

# Part III

# OVERCOMING THE OBSTRUCTIONS TO TRUTH

Great intuitive gifts are given to us to discern the Truth and discover the right path, but we often get confused because we allow our intuition to be covered by a dark veil. We then lose confidence in our perceptive abilities and outsource our thinking to "wiser" persons.

What is the nature of the dark veil that covers our intuition and how can we remove it? The dark veil is sewn by threads of selfishness, conceit, anxiety, complexity, and human opinions. In this part of the book, we will address these five plagues and their obstructive impact on the path to truth.

# CHAPTER 10

# The Elephant in the Room

## Selfishness

*The whole world yearns after freedom, yet each
creature is in love with his chains*
— *Sri Aurobindo*

In the business world, constraint is a term commonly used
to describe obstacles that prevent a company from attaining
its goals. Identifying the greatest constraint is the first step
in turning around a failing company. Instead of trying to fix
or improve every aspect of the company, a good consultant
wisely deploys his resources toward reducing or eliminating
the greatest constraint. The greatest constraint is usually
obvious after careful assessment of the business operations
and, as Greg McKeown put it in his book, *Essentialism:
The Disciplined Pursuit of Less,* by asking the question,
"What is the obstacle that, if removed, would make
most of the other obstacles disappear?"

I once worked at a company where most employees knew that our greatest constraint was the lack of a robust business system. One that enabled trade and contract management, settlements, risk management strategies, and credit and accounting functions. If it had a good business system, many inefficiencies in various departments would be eliminated and inaccurate reporting would be significantly reduced. Rather than give this constraint the attention it deserved by pausing all unnecessary activities and diverting all available resources to implement the new business system, business continued as usual, with each department doing its best with the resources at its disposal. Consultants were hired and attempts were made to implement the business system, but there was no coordinated and focused effort to get the job done promptly. As the implementation timeline dragged on, requiring more meetings and testing without much progress to justify the significant time investment, frustration mounted leaving employees wondering if things will ever get better.

If you were to perform a constraint analysis on yourself as an exercise, what would you discover? What is that key obstacle to your spiritual growth upon which the other obstacles lean for support?

The following tale shows how it is often easier for us to maintain the status quo because it takes concentrated effort to identify and take serious action against our greatest constraint.

Once, many centuries ago, there was a massive ugly tree in the middle of a village. It was known as the Tree of Selfishness because it occupied the most fertile piece of land in the entire region, yet it produced no edible fruits. Its long, thick branches prevented sufficient sunlight from reaching the field of crops planted in the vicinity of its enormous shadow.

One day, a young woman suggested that they uproot the tree, as she could see what a burden it had become to her people. They scoffed at her. Uprooting this massive tree would be backbreaking work, they argued; it would require months of hard labor. The tree had always been there, and the people had learned to live with it. They felt that they would continue to find ways to deal with it and refused to see the wisdom in the young woman's suggestion. Occasionally, they would cut down some of its branches so that more sunlight could reach the struggling crops in the shade underneath the tree. As the years passed, the woman stood by quietly and let them be. She said no more about uprooting the tree.

Generation after generation passed. As the tree grew larger, its heavy branches shaded more and more of the fertile land until the tree nearly blotted out the sun. Food scarcity ensued. The people ran from one expert to another for guidance on how to increase their food production. They would do anything and everything, try all kinds of experiments, read all kinds of books, invent new tools— if only they could find a way to produce enough food to sustain themselves. The people never seriously considered removing the tree, for they refused to see the scourge it had become. All their ancestors had lived with the tree. Stories of the tree had been passed down to them for centuries, so it had become part of their village's identity. They were willing to pay any price and undertake any action, except the very one that would permanently resolve the problem: taking down the ancient tree.

One day, an old farmer found a tablet buried in the ground beside the ancient tree. Inscribed on the stone were instructions on how to remove the tree. It was the work of the young woman who, centuries before, had suggested that her people uproot the tree. Guided from above, she had written down the instructions that must be adhered to by the people to uproot the Tree of Selfishness.

The old man shared this tablet with his neighbors. Faced with starvation, those who still wished to save themselves began the great work of uprooting the massive tree. They were soon weary unto death, for this work required all their strength, but they gradually grew stronger. The more they attacked the root of the tree, the weaker became its influence over them. Seeing its vulnerability, they worked harder and more confidently until the massive tree, which had cast darkness for a thousand years, collapsed to the ground. Freed of this obstruction, a clear path to the invigorating rays of the sun was once again restored to the land. Within a few months, the crops prospered, the air was cleaner, and the people were happy. Only now did they discern the widespread impact of the Tree of Selfishness on all aspects of their former lives.

*\*\**

# Selfishness is a self-imposed blindness because it blocks out spiritual light.

It stifles the luminous spark within us that would otherwise lead us to the greatest happiness. As with the people of this mythic land, selfishness permeates much of our world's activity today. It has been part of our dealings with one another for so long that it is now engrained in our way of life.

Every national anthem I have ever heard speaks of the high ideals of liberty, peace, or brotherhood, and yet none of this is possible where the tree of selfishness lives within us. For world peace, we will do anything and everything, try all kinds of experiments, read all kinds of books, make many speeches, and pay any price, except uprooting the major obstacle that prevents the attainment of peace: selfishness. To address climate change, billions of dollars will be poured into innovative solutions and policies will be enacted to encourage the adoption of renewable sources of energy, but little focus will be paid to addressing the selfish and short-sighted mindset that led to the accelerated warming of our planet. Why is this? As with the people in the Tree of Selfishness story, it is hard to change our well-established behaviors, especially when serious effort is required. It is easier to find solutions that address the symptoms rather than tackle the cause. But these are never lasting solutions. The problems will only resurface in a new form.

Selfishness blocks the inner light that we need to find the path to Truth. Thus, selfishness is one of the greatest obstructions to truth. Our personal and material interests are certainly important, but never at the expense of our conscience. When we ignore our conscience, we betray ourselves, thereby weakening our defenses and exposing ourselves to grave dangers. To attain a higher level of spiritual awareness, we will all find ourselves in circumstances that call us to stretch beyond our comfort zone. Perhaps we may have to challenge long-held beliefs, forfeit financial gain in the short term, or overcome the fear of being too different. By answering this call, we not only help others, but we draw closer to the Almighty Father. The following story gives an example of this.

In the city of Tabriz lived a middle-aged jewelry merchant named Ardashir. He felt a great sense of responsibility for the jewelry store as it had belonged to his family for generations. For this reason, he was strict with his workers and distrustful of them. Workers are innately unreliable and lazy was his belief, and they needed close supervision and discipline. This belief was backed by experience, nineteen years of firsthand experience to be precise. Over the years, he learned to deal with his unreliable workers. Cameras were installed to prevent stealing, fines were established to discourage tardiness and a no-tolerance policy was in place to combat insubordination.

The competitive external struggle with other jewelry stores along with his internal struggle with his workers took a toll on the aging man. He was exhausted! He thought of Babak, one of his best workers who resigned two months ago. "Why do my best workers leave me?" In reflection, he noticed that Babak was no exception, none of his few exceptional workers ever stayed beyond a year.

Ardashir! "One who rules with Truth," this was the meaning of his name. A name he was always so proud to bear. But now Ardashir sounded distant, as if it no longer belonged to him. The constant distrust of his employees had so poisoned this man's heart that he no longer sought the guidance of Truth. In this tender moment, the word "Love" rang out loud and clear. "Assign no task to an employee that you would not perform yourself, first seek the happiness of those under your authority ahead of your prosperity." The floodgates opened, and these words kept flowing. Lastly, he heard… "Do to them as you would like to be done by."

If we cannot be selfless at home or at work. If we only think of what our friend, family, employee, or employer can do for us, it is unrealistic to think we can successfully overcome those pivotal moments that could lead us closer to the path to truth.

The spirit originates from the perfection in paradise. The intellect originates from the gross material world and is thus much more limited in scope than the spirit. With the spirit leading through the intuition and the intellect executing, we can transform the earth into a material paradise. The desire to serve awakens the human spirit and strengthens our connection with our spiritual origin, thus allowing us to pull from the greatest wisdom available to us. The greater connection with our spiritual origin enables us to experience heaven on earth in certain moments of bliss. It is no coincidence that we are filled with inner joyfulness and lightness when engaged in genuine service to others. Noble ideas float our way that are then planned out and executed by the intellect.

"The intuitive mind is a sacred gift, and the rational mind is a faithful servant. We have created a society that honors the servant and has forgotten the gift." - Albert Einstein

We forget and suppress the sacred gift of intuition when we are blindly consumed by the desire to get. The spirit recedes to the background and can no longer offer its light. The intellect then takes center stage. Limited in its scope and lacking the guidance of the spirit, the intellect rationalizes and justifies any means to attain its base ends. Lies and deception become tolerable when disguised as diplomacy. Exploitation becomes defensible when viewed as economic progress. Moral decadence becomes acceptable when promoted as personal liberty.

I have yet to meet a person who does not want to experience a consistent state of inner joy. The only difference between us is what we think will bring about the joy that we all seek. One thinks it is money, another thinks it is family, another thinks it is fame, etc. We pursue what we think will make us joyful, and only after its attainment can we ascertain whether it indeed brings us joy. Our experiences will show us all we need to know regarding this. From our experience, we may discover that true joy is simply a consequence of selfless service. The joy of money is found in the financial freedom it provides to pursue purposeful work wholeheartedly. The joy of family is found in the selfless service of a loved one and the mutual exchange of strengthening radiations. The benefit of fame is the platform it provides to influence other lives positively at a greater scale.

Selfishness may bring transient pleasures, but it makes no one happy in the end. It chokes off the spirit and thereby weakens our connection to the source of all goodness and wisdom—to the source of truth.

# CHAPTER 11

# Pride Comes Before the Fall

## Conceit

*He who seeks knowledge increases day by day; he who seeks the spirit, decreases day by day*
— *Unknown*

There is an account in the Bible in which the Pharisees accuse Christ and His disciples of violating the Sabbath when they see Christ healing a crippled woman. The Sabbath restrictions forbade many forms of physical activity. So the Pharisees wanted to know why Christ was violating this commandment mediated to them by Moses.

The commandment to keep the Sabbath day holy was given to provide people a period of rest and self-reflection to review their lives, or at the very least, the experiences of the past week to draw lessons for their spiritual development. In their rigid, intellectual interpretation of the commandment, the Pharisees had reduced it to merely an abstention from physical activities. They did not understand the spirit of the commandment. In hindsight, it is easy for us to censure the Pharisees for their conceit in challenging Christ. But would we act differently if we were in their shoes? Would an expert or authority in a particular field today welcome the perspective of a novice with superior knowledge, especially if the novice's perspective challenges the beliefs of the so-called expert?

The Pharisees were learned men who dedicated their lives to the study of the Torah. They saw themselves as the spiritual authority of the land. But how well did they understand the messages passed down to them in the Torah? The answer to this question is evident by their constant antagonism toward Christ. Christ's growing influence over the people threatened their power, hence, the reason for their antagonism. Had they truly understood and embodied in spirit the messages of the Torah, they would have been receptive to the words of Christ. They were aware of the prophecy proclaiming the coming of Christ but likely expected the Messiah to come from their ranks. After all, they saw themselves as the true servants of the Creator.

Christ infused the ancient words of the Torah with new life. He explained spiritual principles through parables and proclaimed new teachings that clearly revealed His superior knowledge to any objective listener. Rather than open themselves to this superior knowledge, which was new to them, most of the Pharisees held on to their old, rigid beliefs. They were comfortable in their traditions and enjoyed the authority they exercised over the people as a result of their revered position. A few of them recognized the truth in Christ's words, but most attacked Him vehemently and made His work incredibly difficult. They who claimed to be servants of the Creator were the ones most antagonistic to the Creator's envoy. In their conceit and ignorance, they could not tolerate the sight of an outsider challenging their teachings and threatening their power—even if that outsider was Jesus Christ Himself. Their conceit blocked all objective reasoning.

Like the Pharisees, excessive pride in our limited perceptions prevents any opportunity to expand our understanding. It is healthy to question periodically statements long believed to be true. It is not enough to read and regurgitate the words in spiritual texts. We must bring these words to life spiritually through our experiences, and thereby discover their rightness or their shortcomings. We bring them to life by internalizing them and weaving them into our daily lives.

For example, many nice-sounding things are said about God's love. But if we really internalize and reflect on what love truly means—we will see that the greater part of love is severity. What will become of a football team if the coach rushes to his players and pats them on the back every time they make a mistake? What will become of his players if he does not demand their best effort and mental concentration at every practice? The players will never reach their potential and the team will be unprepared for the challenges that await them during the season. I don't imply that there is no place for tenderness. A wise coach knows the delicate balance between severity and tenderness and knows how to manage the different personalities on his team.

If we expect severity from a good earthly leader, should we expect any less from the Creator of the universe? We have the capacity to go deeper into the words we hear or read in spiritual texts and to find the intended message behind the words. It is indolence to accept a concept or teaching simply out of tradition or because it sounds pleasant. Complacency and pride precede the fall. To be sure of the way, we must test and investigate by closely observing our experiences. Experience alone brings about the right understanding, and thus, conviction.

There is no end to our self-development on earth. In every aspect of life, there is always room for improvement. While on earth, we can never be content with our spiritual condition. We must keep climbing by learning from each experience and improving our ability to recognize the Will of the Creator.

# One of the signs of conceit is the habit of discussing the faults of others.

We may not openly confess this, but by discussing the faults of others, we often think we are superior to them. Rather than quietly learning from the faults of others, we openly criticize and thereby lose the opportunity presented for our growth. Take, for instance, the following conversation between two friends, Fakira and Sodiq.

"Does she see herself? How can she leave her house wearing those tight shorts?" Fakira said to her friend Sodiq after seeing Aisha, their classmate, who was only five feet tall but easily weighed over two hundred pounds. "You would think that losing some weight would be a priority, but she is not even bothered. Does she not realize how much easier her life would be if she freed herself from some of that weight?"

"We all have our lives to live. Let her be," Sodiq casually responded.

**\***

Imagine all the unnecessary weight we carry around in the form of excessive anxieties and worries. It's like mental and emotional obesity. We carry this heavy burden, oblivious to how it affects us spiritually because no time is taken in the middle of our haste for reflection. Imagine how much easier our lives would become if we threw off this excess weight.

With the right perception, Fakira could have gained much from her encounter with Aisha. For she was being shown a picture of her inner state in the form of Aisha. In her pharisaical attitude, she could not see this projection and thereby missed the opportunity presented for spiritual growth. Oftentimes, a similar version of the weaknesses of others that most annoy us also lives within us. Not for nothing do we encounter various experiences over the course of the day; we simply need to make the effort to draw the right lessons from each experience for the sake of our development.

Observe the media, observe the conversations of friends and neighbors, and observe your own conversations. You will see how much time is spent discussing the faults of others. There is more than enough to censure in ourselves, yet we would rather castigate others for their shortcomings.

A man criticizes the hateful actions of a dictator living on the other side of the planet, and yet he himself is easily prone to irritation, anger, and hate. They share the same passions. Does that not make them brothers before the laws of Creation? Would this man act any differently if he were given absolute power?

Another man asserts, "A thief must be severely punished to deter others from doing likewise." Yet he enjoys receiving stolen goods in the form of television shows and magazines that make a business out of revealing private information about celebrities. Does he not play a role in the encouragement of gossip and thievery?

A judge sentences a man who is found guilty of sexual assault, and yet he takes pleasure at the sight of scantily clad women. While the condemned man is publicly forced to face his impurities, the judge secretly continues to harbor his lustful thoughts. Society respects the judge but denounces the convict. Which of them is really more advanced spiritually?

Pause and reflect deeply on these words from the Lebanese poet Kahlil Gibran. "And as a single leaf turns not yellow but with the silent knowledge of the whole tree, so the wrong-doer cannot do wrong without the hidden will of you all." Does this ring true?

Those who break the law and disturb the peace of others should certainly be held accountable. But if we think we are superior to these individuals, that very thought is evidence enough that we are not.

This is not to encourage indifference to the injustices of mankind or recommend that we turn a blind eye to the faults of others. Rather, it calls for some inner reflection.

If in quiet reflection, we have the humility and calmness to set aside the faults of others and focus on ourselves instead, the right lessons to aid our spiritual growth will emerge.

Consider a scenario where someone is betrayed by a friend. Dwelling on the actions of the friend is useless. Reflecting on the relationship with this friend to recognize the signs missed that foreshadowed the betrayal is useful. Becoming aware of these signs will be helpful in the assessment of future friendships and associations. The American poet Maya Angelou once said: "When people show you who they are, believe them the first time." A man at a gathering of friends who listens indifferently as an absent man is being discussed in a bad light will one day be the absent man. The boss who favors ostentatiousness over quiet productivity and promotes employees accordingly will one day watch her company crumble on account of her poor judgment. A woman who observes her partner's rudeness to others on several occasions but takes no strong action to confront him about it will one day be on the receiving end of his rudeness. To the discerning spirit, the present reveals much about our fellow human beings if we only pick up the cues. Those who spend most of their time discussing the faults of others bar themselves from spiritual insights that would otherwise be theirs if they simply turned their critical lens inward. Conceit obstructs truth because it prevents this critical self-assessment.

# CHAPTER 12

# Don't Let Your Tears Blind You

## Anxiety

*The answer during times of doubt is not to walk away from service to others, but to seek it out even more than before*
— *John Wooden*

There is a Yoruba proverb that warns, "When crying, don't let your tears blind you." It simply means that if we give in completely to our fears and sorrows, we only compound the problem and prevent ourselves from seeing the opportunities wrapped in the present. To prosper we must boldly face our current reality, however difficult it may be, and wholeheartedly embrace the opportunities of the present. For only the gifts of the present can make the future brighter. We are called to live well today. If we do so, tomorrow will certainly take care of itself. The following story shows how brooding can take us down a path of great suffering, while just as easily, a cheerful outlook can lift us above all gloominess.

"What's next?" These words escaped Bella Wilson's lips on her drive back home from the University of Wisconsin. Suddenly overcome by sadness and heaviness of heart, she parked on the side of the road to regain her composure.

Her last child, Nathan, was now off to college, and although she had been preparing for this day for months, only now had it become a reality. Since her divorce a decade earlier, all she did revolved around the care of her three children. She loved them and was happy with their progress into adulthood, but she also felt an overwhelming sense of loss and abandonment, a loneliness that was eating her up. As she watched the cars zoom past, with tears dripping slowly down her face, she entertained the thought of joining her beloved mother in the afterlife. "What next? What do I have to look forward to?" It was not that long ago that she graduated from college with great hopes of a future with a loving family and a fulfilling career. All that was behind her now. *How quickly the years go by*, she mused.

Suddenly, her brooding was interrupted by the sight of an old, green Isuzu pickup truck that barely made it off the road and parked right in front of her car. Something was obviously wrong, so she wiped away her tears and got out of her car to go ask whether the stranded man needed help. His truck had run out of gas. She cheerfully offered to help the stranger. He was extremely grateful for her help in driving him to a gas station to buy gas and bringing him back to his vehicle. As she helped the stranger fill up his gas tank, so did he unknowingly fill up her joy tank.

Bella's service to the stranger erased her previous anxiety about living alone without her children. She had found the answer to her question "What's next?" Every single human being is given the opportunity, every day, to find true joy through service. This simple realization was helpful to Bella because what she had feared with Nathan's departure was the loss of joy. Now she knew that joy was abundantly available through genuine service. Regardless of our circumstances, we all can contribute something to the enhancement of our environment. This is the spirit needed to overcome adversity.

Many have high aspirations for their lives, but we sometimes find ourselves in jobs or circumstances that are quite different from those aspirations. The years go by, and the melancholy memory of those unfulfilled aspirations makes us sad. We may console ourselves by rationalizing that our earlier aspirations are unattainable in the "real world." But the aspirations never really go away. In the dissatisfaction with our circumstances, we sometimes resort to complaining about everything that is wrong around us.

Life will be painfully difficult if we do not take control of our lives. Just as weeds rise to occupy empty garden space, so will negative thoughts assail us if we don't channel our energy in a constructive and purposeful direction. Complaining is a great danger because it only compounds our anxieties. The more we complain about our problems, the more we prevent ourselves from receiving the needed help. A good example of this is illustrated by the tale of the Master and the repentant harlot.

Many centuries ago in the Middle East, a man in simple garb walked the streets. He was the shining light and staff for all those who yearned to be true human beings.

One day a woman condemned as a harlot by society, and thus treated with the utmost disrespect, came to the end of her road. She could no longer go on living as a pariah and saw in this great man, whom they called "Master," her only hope for a better existence.

She stood at the back of a large crowd for hours as the Master addressed the multitude and tended to people who came to him for healing. She struggled to make her way through the crowd to get closer to him, so she waited until the crowd had dispersed to seek his help. As the Master and his close companions turned to leave, she called out and ran toward him. She was speechless when she stood before him and bowed her head.

"You wish to speak to me? Tell me what you want," the Master said.

She lost her shyness and said in a weary voice, "See how they all despise me, Master! I cannot speak in their presence. Indeed, they make it impossible for me to lead a different life. They always remind me of my sin and shun me wherever they see me. They take their children away when I walk in the street and threaten to stone me."

The Master said nothing. He walked quietly on, and the woman remained by his side without any objection from him. He left the town, and still, the woman walked by his side. The hours went by.

At last the Master halted and said, "What do you hope for from me that you do not go home?"

"A word of advice, Master."

"When I asked what you wanted, you did not say. You made accusations! You had nothing but complaints and lamentations. That is why I could not help you. Now I will give you advice. Go to another country and begin the new life for which you long. Work from morning until night in order to forget the past. You are young and can still make up for all that you have neglected."

***

Daily, hourly, Creation says the same to us: *Tell me what you want.* We respond by the nature of our innermost thoughts, words, and deeds. Help cannot reach the person who whines and complains; it simply finds no way to penetrate a closed heart. However, help unfailingly reaches those who make the effort to seek humbly and live honorably, often coming when least expected.

No one is immune from hardship, but we all can face it courageously if we so choose. Anxiety is self-sabotage. It denotes a lack of trust in our abilities to connect to the helpful radiations of the Creator that are always present.

# Channel your anxiety into useful service and you will be on your way to higher ground.

The great composer, Ludwig van Beethoven, struggled to come to terms with his deafness. He wrote the following in 1802 as he was formulating Symphony No. 3: "But what humiliation when any one beside me heard a flute in the far distance, while I heard nothing, or when others heard a shepherd singing, and I still heard nothing! Such things brought me to the verge of desperation, and well-nigh caused me to put an end to my life. Art! Art alone deterred me. Ah! How could I possibly quit the world before bringing forth all that I felt it was my vocation to produce?" The total commitment to something higher, to give something of value to his fellow human beings is what strengthened him in his moments of despair. The path to truth and happiness is available to all who seek it. We need not be anxious or fearful if we just do our best to live well today. When crying, don't let your tears blind you.

CHAPTER 13

# Complexity Masks Ignorance

It is very simple to be happy, but it is
very difficult to be simple
— *Rabindranath Tagore*

Have you ever tried to explain a concept to a child only to discover that you didn't understand it as well as you thought you did? The ability to explain a complex process simply is the truest sign of understanding.

Just as you would be wary of a salesman who must resort to using big words to explain the benefit of his product, so must you be wary of complex explanations or practices in your search for the path to truth. The path to truth is simple. The following story highlights the power of practicing simplicity with constant repetition.

Prompted by his mother's recent heart attack, Santiago began an exercise routine with a trainer at his local gym. His mother's heart attack was caused by a buildup of plaque in her coronary arteries, decreasing the blood flow to her heart. His seriousness was evident by his diligent effort day after day, despite the soreness of his body after each workout. He expected to make great strides and was disappointed at having lost only six pounds in the first month. "These exercises are not effective," he sometimes said to his trainer. Slowly, his enthusiasm waned until he eventually terminated his appointments with the trainer.

He began looking online for more complex routines. He would begin one routine only to stop it after a few weeks if he had not attained his desired weight loss objective. And so it went for two years . . . the thrill of a new routine, practicing it diligently for a few weeks, subsequently followed by apathy and the longing for a newer, more effective routine. He never practiced any routine long enough to fully reap its benefits.

Leaving the grocery store one morning, Santiago saw a familiar face but could not quite place the person, who said, "Long time, Santiago, how have you been? We have not seen you at the gym in a while." Santiago instantly recognized the voice of his former workout partner, Frederick, who had stayed with the trainer after Santiago left. Frederick was almost unrecognizable; he looked slimmer, and his belly was flatter than Santiago remembered. Santiago stood before his old friend in disbelief. He was astonished by his remarkable progress and realized his mistake in prematurely leaving the trainer.

*\*\*

# True greatness lies in simplicity. It requires the firm will to do simple things consistently.

Regarding spiritual growth, the incessant desire to acquire new knowledge without putting previously gained insights into consistent practice is indolence disguised as earnest effort.

We often fail to recognize great wisdom when it is clothed in simple words. For example, the guidance to purify thy thoughts, to love thy neighbor, and to know thyself. We have heard these words so often that we tend to overlook their great significance. They are the basics. If we only focused on these basics, all religions would merge into the faith of love. What good is it to know the entire Bible or the Koran by heart if one's thoughts are governed by selfishness? It is through the consistent practice of the basics that real knowledge expands, not through constantly searching for more books and sages.

With the consistent practice of the basics, the right books and circumstances will emerge at the appropriate hour without externally seeking them out. To purify thy thoughts, to love thy neighbor, to know thyself requires constant effort. We cannot avoid this step.

As with Frederick, sticking to the basics may seem plain, but it will get us to the goal. Patience is required. Patience cannot be sustained without confidence. That is why the knowledge of the nature of the Creator discussed in the first part of the book is essential, for it gives us confidence. Earlier, we talked about how a mango seed can only yield mangoes. The fruit may not arrive when we want it, but it will eventually arrive if the seed we plant is consistently nurtured.

Have you ever watched a flower closely to identify the exact moment it blooms? The blooming is a gradual process. We see the bud closed one day and opened the next, but the actual moment of transformation is hardly discernible to the naked eye. It is the same with our spiritual blooming. While in the middle of a major transformational change, one is rarely aware of it. With the increasing spiritual knowledge gained from our daily experiences, the spark of light within us gradually expands more and more until it blooms and permeates our whole being. Patience! The simple seemingly insignificant everyday activities are more significant than we may realize. As Abd-ru-shin admonishes in *The Grail Message*: "If you deal exclusively and earnestly with what is good, all else follows of its own accord."

Our high aspirations will be attained. Their accomplishment is the result of small, simple things done well and consistently. Complex rituals and extreme measures are not the way.

# CHAPTER 14

# A Harmful Crutch

## Human Opinions

Fools and intelligent people are equally harmless, half-
fools and half-sages, these are the most dangerous of all
— *Johann Wolfgang von Goethe*

The above words of German playwright Johann Wolfgang
von Goethe have been proven true, time and time again.
We see evidence of this throughout history. The partially
false descriptions of the Creator perpetuated by half-sages
over the centuries have been damaging to our spiritual
development and our understanding of spiritual law. It
has weakened trust in the omnipotence of the Creator.
Where understanding was lacking, these half-sages added
their personal opinions about the Creator, which were then
passed on as absolute truth to future generations. The lack
of logic in these explanations leaves the objective seeker
confused, which may lead him to give up the search entirely.

We discussed the perfection and orderliness of Creation
in the first part of the book. The dictionary defines

"perfection" as "excellent or complete beyond practical or theoretical improvement." "Perfect" is the appropriate adjective for describing the Creator's work because His work is excellent and beyond improvement. Every aspect of His Creation works extremely efficiently, checks and balances are in place, and nothing falls through the cracks. Only what is perfect endures for billions of years. Great empires rise and fall, but the perfect order of the universe continues.

Taking an extreme position, either of fanaticism or indifference, when it comes to beliefs is detrimental to the discovery of truth, because it precludes taking a calm, neutral stance of objectivity. The manipulation of truth, even slightly, to suit human interests immediately robs truth of its purity and makes it a lie. Under the banner of "truth," thousands have marched to war on behalf of religions that profess love. Partly true statements are frequently dressed up and presented as the truth to sway congregations, voters, customers, employees, and people from all walks of life. Teachings and books arise from all sides to enlighten us and show us the path to truth. How do we discern truth from half-truths (lies)?

We will address this question. But first, let us take as an example the differing opinions of the earth's shape in earlier times. Until a certain point in the history of mankind, the notion that the earth was flat was incontestable. The experts of the time disseminated this view, and those interested in the subject went along with the flat earth theory. After all, the experts must have known what they were talking about.

We now know, of course, that the earth is spherical. But what else do we consider as a fact today that in years hence will be discovered to be only an opinion? How much of what we deem correct will later prove to be wrong? In the face of ignorance, amid all confusion, despite our assertions, the truth stands!

We cannot personally investigate every topic, but we ought to investigate areas that directly impact our well-being. When it comes to the great eternal questions of life, which are of paramount importance to every human being (*Who am I? Why am I here? What happens after death?*), it is not uncommon today to hear the phrase, "You have your truth. I have mine." This is said as if truth were a subjective thing, as if it could vary according to the whims and feelings of human beings. Truth, being unchangeable and eternal, is.

Five times five will always come to twenty-five. The Spanish word for the number "five" differs from the English word for "five." But that does not change the fact that five times five will always be twenty-five. By analogy, people from different parts of the world may have their own words for certain spiritual concepts and entities. But the truth remains unchanged everywhere in the world. Otherwise, it would not be truth. Truth belongs to no creed or religion. The helpful radiations of the Creator stand unconcerned yet ever watchful. They stand unconcerned as to whether we discover the path to truth, yet they are ever watchful and reveal their light to those who humbly and earnestly seek it with a pure heart.

Listen dispassionately as people engage in heated discussions about religion under the illusion that they are defending the truth, when in fact they are only defending their fallible opinions. He who walks in the light of truth does not argue with others about the worthiness of his convictions. Their worth will shine from his eyes, his warmth, his every movement, and his interaction with all living creatures.

The blind adoption of human opinions guarantees mediocrity at best because by doing so we deprive ourselves of the growth that comes from personal investigation.

On a Sunday evening on July 15, 1838, standing before the senior class of Divinity College, Ralph Waldo Emerson said the following:

"Let me admonish you, first of all, to go alone; to refuse the good models, even those which are sacred in the imagination of men and dare to love God without mediator or veil. Friends enough you shall find who will hold up to your emulation Wesleys and Oberlins, Saints and Prophets.

Thank God for these good men, but say, "I also am a man." Imitation cannot go above its model. The imitator dooms himself to hopeless mediocrity. The inventor did it, because it was natural to him, and so in him it has a charm. In the imitator, something else is natural, and he bereaves himself of his own beauty, to come short of another man's."

Dick Fosbury's story reveals the wisdom of Mr. Emerson's words. In 1963, the sixteen-year-old Fosbury was the worst high jumper on his high school track team. Even with his best efforts, the young man did not make much progress using the standard model of high jumping at the time, which was called the western roll. One day, he began experimenting with alternative techniques to see if there was a better approach that would help him jump higher over the high jump bar. In order to lift his hips above the bar, he ignored the prevailing model and did what came naturally to him. He moved his shoulders back as he approached the bar and jumped over it backward. He cleared the bar that day with this approach, and from then on, he began working on improving his new technique.

Fast-forward five years . . . Dick Fosbury introduced his unorthodox technique to the track and field world at the 1968 Olympic Games in Mexico, where he won the gold medal. His technique of jumping backward, known as the Fosbury Flop, is now the standard technique used by high jumpers around the world. Dick Fosbury had the *awareness* that there had to be a better way that worked for him. He was not trying to change the sport of high jump but simply trying to find a method that would elevate him higher over the bar. Had he just imitated the prevailing century-old technique of high jumping, he would have, in Emerson's words, "bereaved himself of his own beauty to come short of another man's." Instead, by doing what was natural to him, he took the high jump to new heights with his more graceful and effective technique.

Each of us must find our own way to the path of truth. We must find a method that continually elevates us over the bar of spiritual complacency. Just as our scientific knowledge keeps growing and evolving with every discovery, so must our spiritual insights continually expand. For this to happen, we must question things we have long taken for granted to be true and seek to confirm them through our experiences and observations. As with Dick Fosbury, it may take years to find and develop a unique approach that helps our spirit soar. But this is time well spent because only personal and perpetual effort can keep us aloft.

After that brief detour, let's go back to the question of how to discern truth from half-truths (lies). Human opinions vary widely about the path to truth. There is so much written on the subject that it can be overwhelming. Dear friend, take comfort in these words from *The Grail Message*:

"He who bears within himself the firm volition for what is good, and strives to give purity to his thoughts, has already found the way to the Highest! All else will then be added unto him. This requires neither books, nor spiritual strain; neither asceticism, nor solitude. He will become sound in body and soul, freed from all pressure of morbid pondering; for all exaggeration is harmful. You are meant to be human beings, not hothouse plants which through one-sided cultivation succumb to the first puff of wind!

Awake! Look around you! Listen to your inner voice! That alone can open the way!"

These words help us answer the question of how to discern truth from half-truths. By closely observing our surroundings and listening to our inner voice, we will find the way. But we must first shatter the walls we have built up that prevent us from hearing our inner voice. Ridding ourselves of the obstacles of selfishness, conceit, and anxiety, as discussed earlier in Part 3, will shatter the walls and give purity to our thoughts. By striving to rid ourselves of these plagues, we will grow in our ability to hear our inner voice more clearly and thus discover the path to truth.

Frequent idle talk is another plague to be mindful of because it has the effect of dissipating our energy, not to mention the fact that it is difficult to listen within while constantly talking. A practical example of this is illustrated by the following encounter between a bank manager and his employee.

Iris walked into her manager's office seeking permission to take the next two days off. Mr. Noble happily consented.

"How is it that I already knew her request before she had voiced it?" he whispered to himself as Iris left his office.

Mr. Noble was not new at sensing events before they happened. Just yesterday, he had correctly predicted who the caller would be before picking up his ringing phone. He had previously dismissed such events as flukes, but the multiple occurrences over the past month proved otherwise and induced him to investigate further.

He decided to write down everything he could remember about his state of being on these occasions. He realized that his intuition was sharpest at times when his spirit was filled completely with thoughts of helping others and when he spoke only out of necessity. The concentration of his thoughts on service to others freed him of himself, while his practice of silence strengthened his connection with his inner voice.

Armed with this knowledge, the importance of guarding against dissipating his energy by minimizing worthless activities and idle talk became clear to him.

*\*\**

Frequent idle chatter weakens the depth of our perceptive abilities. The age-old admonition to conquer the tongue has been bequeathed to us. "Silence is golden," we are told. We may not always be able to control our thoughts, but we can control our tongues. Try it. Speak as if your every word were a seed planted in fertile soil that will germinate, and you will see for yourself the impact of this warning on your well-being. The stronger the connection with our inner voice becomes, the easier it becomes to discern truth from half-truths.

In a world where we have instantaneous access to information on practically any topic, there is a tendency to accept blindly the opinions and findings of experts in their given field. Although this can be helpful, it can become a harmful crutch if it induces a state of indolence.

A wise patient would follow the orders of his doctor but would also diligently observe the effects of his doctor's prescribed medication on himself.

If it is helpful, he will continue the medication. But if it proves to have harmful side effects, he will proceed with caution. You may decide to follow the spiritual guidance of a mentor or a sacred text, but diligently observe its effect on your state of being. Are you expanding inwardly with new spiritual insights from your experiences? Or are you stagnating and just repeating the words of others?

"Awake! Look around you! Listen to your inner voice! That alone can open the way!"

## Overcoming the Obstructions to Truth

Everything has been so wonderfully arranged that we just need to go with the flow. Externally, we are the recipients of Nature's generous gifts. Internally, the desire for inner joy, which is an innate characteristic of every human spirit, nudges us toward supreme bliss. Why, then, do we obstruct this flow? And how can we remove the obstacles we have placed on our path? We do so by understanding the nature of the obstructions so we can more clearly identify and overcome them.

*Selfishness* – Are your actions more often guided by the desire to serve or the desire to receive? The desire to serve awakens the spirit and strengthens our connection to higher realms, thus allowing us to partake in the pure and abiding joy prevalent above. The desire to receive, however, often chains us more closely to the low limits of the earth.

*Conceit* – Are you secure enough to reassess your strongly held positions, or do you fear opposing views? Do you quietly learn from the failings of others, or do you openly discuss their faults? Those who spend their time discussing the faults of others block spiritual insights that would otherwise be theirs if they simply turned their critical lens inward.

*Anxiety* – Are you constantly worrying about the past or the future? Only in the present can we act to improve our condition. Anxiety is self-sabotage because it only compounds our problem, and it saps our precious time and energy in the present.

*Complexity* – True greatness lies in simplicity. Learn to do simple things consistently—everything else will naturally unfold at the appropriate time.

*Human Opinions* – Are you quick to repeat the opinions of others, or do you think before speaking? The blind adoption of human opinions guarantees mediocrity at best, because by doing so, we deprive ourselves of the growth that comes from personal investigation.

*The Little Things in Action:*

Adopt the practice of asking yourself these three questions before you speak.

Is it true?

Is it good?

Is it useful?

# Epilogue

Earnest, consistent effort is required to change a mindset that has long been shaped by the short-sighted intellect. My hope is that the contents shared will spur you to look about you with new eyes, and that the increasing understanding of the fundamental principles evident all around us in Nature will help you arrange your life in a manner that is in harmony with all existence.

To help bring some of the concepts discussed in this book to life through practical application, I invite you to participate in an exercise.

### HONEST ASSESSMENT

Like a giant oak tree, stand firmly in the knowledge that you reap what you sow. In other words, that your current condition is the result of seeds once sowed by none other than yourself. With this mindset, review your life up to this moment. Let the pivotal experiences of your past come to the fore and see how these experiences shape your current mindset. Write down the attribute you most credit for the successes you have enjoyed and the attribute most responsible for your setbacks and self-doubts.

## DECIDE

Give thanks to The Creator for the gift of the present moment and the opportunity it provides to embark upon the wonderful quest of awakening to the awareness of the great abilities within you. Decide to embark on this quest. Do not take this decision lightly for it will require all your powers of concentration and the formation of new habits. It will prove difficult at first until it becomes second nature. Do not begin until you are committed to sticking with it for seven days. If you should falter, begin again for another seven days.

## SEVEN-DAY CHALLENGE

Let beauty be your guide in everything you say and do for the next seven days. To help you in this, consider the following guidance.

Know Thyself: From your honest self-assessment, remember the attribute you most credit for your successes and call on this strength daily. Reflect on the attribute most detrimental to your ascent and write down how you plan to neutralize it.

Eliminate: Think of your thoughts as your greatest resource (greater than money), as an investment in the subject you choose to dwell upon. Invest wisely. Eliminate everything that does not contribute to awakening the beautiful gifts slumbering within you. Minimize all aimlessness – aimless internet browsing, aimless television watching, aimless outings, aimless talk. This will be hard because we've grown accustomed to seeking distractions to pass the time. Rest and recreation are important but be intentional in the activities you engage in during your leisure hours. More on this in the next guidance.

Prepare and Act: Take control of the day by preparing for it the night before. Preview the day ahead and jot down what you want to accomplish that day. It could be one simple task. The important thing is to get in the habit of previewing the day the night before. During these seven days, give more of yourself than ever before, at home, at work, at school. Seek to make your environment more beautiful. Fill your leisure hours with creative works or activities that inspire beauty and well-being. Remember that the sun's rays do not burn until brought to a focus. Focus its rays on beauty.

After the seven days are over, you will have discovered from first-hand experience that it is possible to truly live well. The awareness of all that you could contribute to your community, with a more prudent use of your time, will become clearer to you. And if you wish to extend this practice beyond seven days,  you will advance in your understanding of true beauty and will grow more and more in its likeness. Each day will then become a blessing to you!

The help of the Almighty Father surrounds us and will see us through any difficulty... if we do not shy away from this ennobling work of purifying ourselves through cultivating beauty in all we say and do. His Light of Truth is available to all true seekers.

# Notes

Abd-ru-shin, *In the Light of Truth: The Grail Message* (Vomperberg, Tyrol: Alexander Bernhardt Publishing Co., 2011) , p.10, 32-33, 971.

Richard Steinpach, *How Can God Allow Such Things?* (Mount Vernon, OH: Grail Foundation Press, 1996).

Clark Glenn, *The Man Who Tapped the Secret of the Universe* (Naples, FL: Mockingbird Press LLC, 2022), p. 13-14.

Damian Carrington, "Humans Just 0.01% of all life but has destroyed over 80% of wildmammals- Study." May 21, 2018. Accessed March 21, 2022 https://www.theguardian.com/environment/2018/may/21/human-race-just-001-of-all-life-but-has-destroyed-over-80-of-wild-mammals-study

Andrew Carnegie, *The Autobiography of Andrew Carnegie* (London: Constable and Co. Ltd., 1920), ch 4, p.46.

Solomon, Maynard (1980). "On Beethoven's Creative Process: A Two-Part Invention". *Music & Letters* 61 (3/4), p. 273.

Orison Swett Marden, *How they Succeeded: Life Stories of Successful Men Told by Themselves* (Boston: Lothrop Publishing Company, 1901), p.7.

Greg McKeown, *Essentialism: The Disciplined Pursuit of Less* (New York: Crown Publishing Group, 2014), ch 16, p.190.

Kahlil Gibran, *Collected Works of Kahlil Gibran* (New Delhi: Fingerprint Publishing, 2023), p. 31.

Alexander Wheelock Thayer, *Thayer's Life of Beethoven, Part II* (New Jersey: Princeton University Press, 1967).

Ralph Waldo Emerson and Earl Morse Wilbur, *The Divinity School Address.* Centenary edition (Boston: American Unitarian Association, 1938).

# Acknowledgments

To The Creator for the gift of His Word and this
opportunity of service.

To my parents, Olufemi and Ibilola Bayode for the
background and encouragement that equipped me for
such an endeavor; your sacrifice made this possible.
I thank you. Owe meh, special thanks for devoting
your precious predawn hours to read and critique my
many earlier versions. Your steady supportive presence
throughout this project has been invaluable.

To the best editor I could have hoped for, Kendra
Langeteig. Your thoughtful suggestions and masterful
editing skills were of tremendous value. Thank you.

# About the Author

Oluwaseun Bayode is a writer who seeks out stories that simplify the seeming complexities of life. He writes extensively on little everyday experiences that provide insights into the great spiritual questions of life. From his experiences, he is discovering that the answers to the great questions of life need not be a mystery; they often lie amid our everyday experiences.